Allyn and Bacon

Quick Guide to the Internet for Health

1998 Edition

Michael N. Olpin

Concord College

Allyn and Bacon

Boston • London • Toronto • Sydney • Tokyo • Singapore

Macintosh is a registered trademark of Apple Computer, Inc.

Microsoft is a registered trademark of Microsoft Corporation. Windows, Windows95, and Microsoft Internet Explorer are trademarks of Microsoft Corporation.

Netscape Navigator and the Netscape Navigator logo are registered trademarks of Netscape Communications Corporation

Sprint is a registered trademark of Sprint Communications Company L.P. Sprint Internet Passport is a service mark of Sprint Communications Company L.P.

ISBN 0-205-27941-4

Printed in the United States of America

10   9   8   7   6   5   4   3   01   00   99   98   97

Contents

Sprint Installation Instructions

Part One   Introduction to the Internet

Part Two   Address Book to Health Websites

Get Connected Now!

Load, click and cruise on the Internet with Sprint Internet Passport (SM) for news, information, entertainment and much more. With Sprint Internet Passport, you get full-service, direct Internet access from Sprint, friendly customer service support on-line or by phone 24 hours a day, seven days a week. You'll be able to easily browse around the World Wide Web, and you'll also receive one E-mail account for communicating with family, friends and colleagues. In addition when you get connected with Sprint Internet Passport, you'll receive full access to more than 18,000 Usenet newsgroups, local service from more than 200 U.S. cities (more planned in 1997) and reliable service from one of the Internet's largest carriers.

Pricing for Sprint Internet Passport is $19.95 a month for unlimited use,* or you can pay only for the hours you use at a rate of $1.50 per hour. For your convenience, we'll bill your VISA®, MasterCard® or American Express®.

Just double click on the Sprint icon to start your Internet experience.

Sprint Installation Instructions

DO NOT INSTALL SOFTWARE until you have read the Software License agreement which appears on the CD.

If you currently use Netscape® Navigator as your Internet browser, Sprint Internet Passport will automatically overwrite that software. However, with just a little extra care and effort, Sprint Internet Passport will nicely coexist on your system with your current software. More information and details on the exact steps necessary to preserve your current configuration can be found at http://www.sprint.com/passport, or you can call us at 1-800-786-1400.

*Nation-wide 800 Access Number includes surcharge of $4.80 per hour if local service is not available in your area.

Windows® 3.1 Users

1. Insert the *Sprint Internet Passport* installation CD into your CD-ROM drive.

2. In *Program Manager* or *File Manager,* select *File* from the menu bar, and then select Run.

3. In the *Command Line* field, type *D:\INSTALL* (where D: represents the drive letter of your CD-ROM).

4. Click *OK,* then follow the on-screen prompts to complete the software setup. When you're prompted to do so, allow setup to restart Windows®.

5. When restart is complete, double-click on the *Sprint Internet Passport Account Setup* icon in the *Sprint Internet Passport* program group.

6. Follow the on-screen prompts to set up your *Sprint Internet Passport* account.

7. When registration is completed, double-click on the *Sprint Internet Passport* icon in the *Sprint Internet Passport* program group.

8. Click *Dial.*

You're ready to begin!

Windows95® Users

1. If you have never been on-line before, be sure to have your Windows95® diskettes or *Sprint Internet Passport* CD handy.

2. Insert the *Sprint Internet Passport* installation CD into your CD-ROM drive. On most systems, the setup process will begin automatically within about 10 seconds.

3. If the setup program doesn't begin automatically, click the *Start* button on your Task Bar and then click *Run.* In the *Run* window, type

D:\INSTALL (where *D:* represents the drive letter of your CD-ROM) and click *OK*.

4. Follow the on-screen prompts to complete the software setup. If you're prompted for a Windows95® diskette, place the required diskette in *Drive A:*; if you're prompted for the Windows95® CD, remove the *Sprint Internet Passport* CD from your CD-ROM drive and insert your Windows95® CD. If you're prompted to do so, allow set up to restart your computer.

5. Double-click the *Sprint Internet Passport Account Setup* icon in the *Navigator* window.

6. Follow the on-screen prompts to set up your Sprint Internet Passport account.

7. Once registration is completed, double-click on the *Dial Sprint Internet Passport* icon on your desktop to connect to Sprint Internet Services.

8. If the password field is blank (no stars), enter your password.

9. Click Connect.

10. Double-click the *Sprint Internet Passport* icon on your desktop to launch the Sprint Internet Passport Browser (Netscape Navigator).

You're ready to begin!

Macintosh Users

1. Insert the Sprint Internet Passport installation CD into your CD-ROM drive.

2. The *Sprint Internet Passport* window will appear on your desktop. Inside this window, double-click the *Installer* icon.

3. Follow the on-screen prompts to complete the software setup. Be sure to take the default settings. (Note that default settings are outlined in black on your screen.)

4. When setup is complete, you will be prompted to restart your computer. Click on *Restart*.

5. When restart is complete, the Account Setup window appears. Click on the *Next* arrow in the Account Setup window.

6. Follow the on-screen prompts to set up your Sprint Internet Passport account.

   During Account Setup, your computer will attempt to connect to the registration service to open your account. *If you are using Macintosh System 7.1,* you will be prompted to restart your computer. Click on Restart. When restart is complete, the Account Setup window appears. Click on the *Connect Now* arrow to continue with Account Setup.

7. When registration is complete, you will be prompted to restart your computer. Click on *Restart.*

8. When restart is complete, double-click on the *Sprint Internet Passport* icon in the Sprint Internet Passport window. *FreePPP* will connect you to Sprint Internet Services, and the Sprint Internet Passport browser will launch.

You're ready to begin!

Exiting your Sprint Internet Passport Account

If you're using Windows® 3.1

- Close *Sprint Internet Passport (Netscape Navigator)* by clicking on *File* and then clicking on *Exit.*
- Close any other open Internet client applications (e.g., IRC, FTP, and Telnet sessions).
- Disconnect from *Sprint Internet Passport* by clicking the *Disconnect* button in the *Sprint Internet Dialer* box.

If you're using Windows95®

- Close *Sprint Internet Passport (Netscape Navigator)* by clicking on *File* and then clicking on *Exit.*
- A message will come up stating that there are open modem connections. Choose "yes" to disconnect from the Internet.

- Close any other open Internet client applications (e.g., IRC, FTP, and Telnet sessions).
- Check to make sure there is no button on the Task Bar labeled *Connected to Sprint Internet.* If there is, click on it to bring up the *Sprint Dialer Dialogue* box and click on the *Disconnect* button.

If you're using a Macintosh

- Close *Sprint Internet Passport (Netscape Navigator).*
- Double-click on the FreePPP Setup icon in the Sprint Internet Passport folder.
- Click Disconnect.

Notes

Be sure to record your:

- Dial Access Number
- Sprint Internet Passport Password
- E-mail Address
- Sprint Internet Passport Log-in ID

A README file has been included on your Sprint Internet Passport CD. Windows® 3.X users can find it here: *D:\WIN.31\DISK5\README.TXT* (where D: represents your CD-ROM drive). Windows95® users can access the file by clicking on Start, Clicking on Run, typing *D:\WIN.95\DISK5\README.TXT* (where D: represents your CD-ROM drive), and clicking OK.

For Macintosh users, the *README.txt File* can be found in the Sprint Internet window on the CD.

Your software will automatically search for and attempt to identify your modem. However, if setup encounters difficulties, you may need to identify your modem manually. See the *README.txt File* for more information. Be sure to verify your pricing plan selection.

Be sure your registration address matches your credit card billing address. If your credit card company uses ZIP+4, it is important that you include the extra 4 digits.

If you live in an area where local calls can span two or more area codes, you may want to modify the 1+Area Code settings in your dialer. See the *README.txt File* for more information.

Please review all the numbers available to help ensure your modem dialer is set for a local call. If you are unsure if a number is a local call, check with your local telephone company. Please note that in some areas, a call may be considered long distance, even though it does not require dialing a "1" or "0".

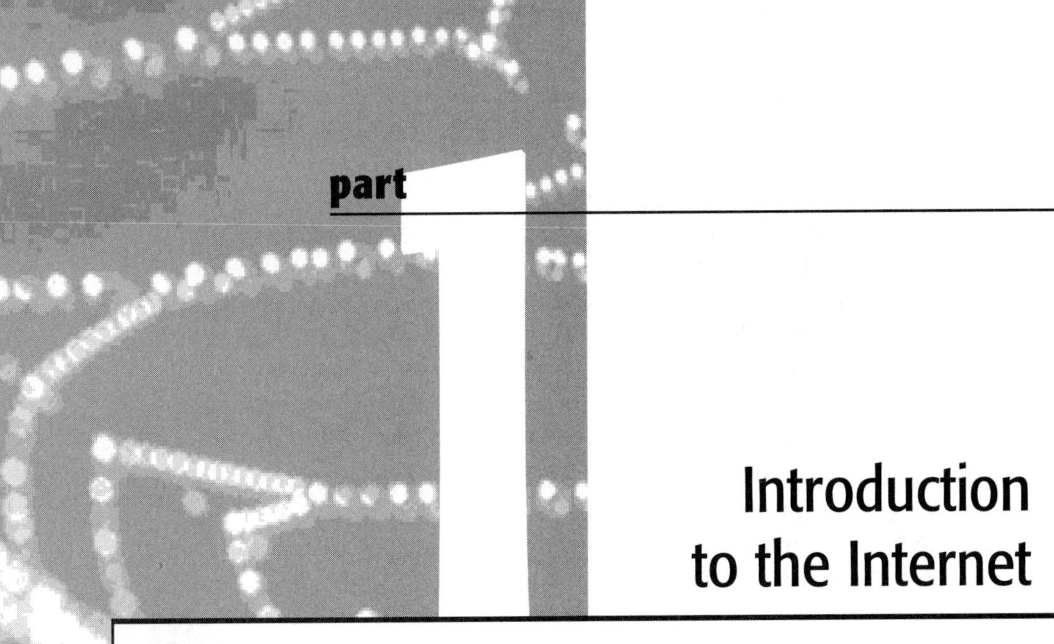

Introduction to the Internet

The Internet—Communication in the '90s

The Internet is a loose affiliation of computers and computer networks. These networks range in size from small, one-computer operations of individual users and small businesses and to the super-sized networks at large corporations and universities.

Who's in Charge Here?

You can think of the Internet as a kind of United Nations, serving only to facilitate the rules by which information is passed from one member to another. The Internet is nothing more than a few committees who establish the rules and languages by which the computers in the member networks talk to each other. Just as the United Nations does not control what goes on within the member countries, there is no organization called the "Internet" that controls what goes on inside each member network.

The Internet is also international in scope and no single government controls it. On one hand this near anarchy has allowed the Internet to grow at an unbelievable rate, but on the other hand the lack of a governing body means that the Internet is a bit like the old Wild West—anything and everything goes, and there's no sheriff to keep law and order.

The Information Explosion

Information relating to health, wellness, health care, and medicine abounds on the Internet. Websites relating to any aspect of health are available with a few mouse clicks. What formerly took hours of searching for information from libraries can now be found in minutes. In former times, contacting colleagues to discuss important ideas required either a long distance phone call or a letter. Now, the Internet allows easy and immediate transmission of these ideas, effortlessly. Like-minded people from all over the world can now discuss ideas, pose questions, and receive new information at lightning speed, literally. The Internet has allowed health information to move to a new and very exciting level of distribution.

With the arrival of the Internet, people looking for health information can find it at every level. For the second grader who wants to learn about the differences between a fruit and a vegetable, it takes little time to find appropriate Web sites to gather this information. For the high school student who needs to write a report on the global situation of HIV and AIDS, information is readily available on the Internet. Similarly, for the scholarly researcher who is looking for information to support a theory on which to build a research study, the avenues are available on the Internet to find this type of information. The Internet has information relevant to every level of learning and there is almost no end to the quantity as well.

Significance for Communication, Education and Research

The Internet has quickly turned into an ocean of information for anyone who wants to know more about any aspect of health. A quick peek at any search engine (a Web site that allows you to search for something on the Internet) such as *Yahoo!* or AltaVista will quickly give us an idea of its immense size. For example, if we point our browser in the direction of the Lycos A2Z search engine (more about browsers a bit later) and then click on the words "Health and Medicine" we immediately move to a page that lists the following topics: Alternative Medicine, Death & Dying, Dentistry, Disabilities, Environmental Medicine, Ethics & Legal Issues in Health, Family Medical Almanac, Family Medicine, Hospitals, & Clinics, Human Sexuality, Illnesses & Disorders, Medical History, Medical Insurance, Medical Research, Mental Health, Nutrition & Wellness, Occupational Medicine, Parenting, Pharmaceuticals, Professional Medicine, Public Health, and Public Policy Issues relating to health. Clicking on any of these topic areas will take us to long lists of Web sites relating to those topic areas.

You may be asking yourself, "If there is so much information out there, where does a person begin when researching a subject or just wanting to know one particular idea." For example, you may just want to know how many grams of fat are in the dinner you just ate at McDonalds. With a little bit of patience and following the steps and Internet addresses found in this book, you will be surprised how quickly you can find that for which you are looking.

Health topics on the information highway come from many different avenues. Many Web sites are designed for the sole purpose of giving out information. For example, a Web page dealing with weight control may tell you little more than data on foods and the various nutrients that are found in the foods. Other, more elaborate Web sites on weight control may have you fill out a questionnaire and then, based on your individual information, give you a printout of such information that is a bit more tailored to your needs. For example, it might let you know about the number of calories you need to consume daily to maintain, lose or gain weight. Considering your questionnaire, it may tell you how much exercise you ought to doing during a typical week. It may give you pointers about what to look for on a food label to keep your intake of fats and sugars at a desirable level. Some Web sites are more interactive than others. The quality of the health related Web sites are as varied as the content.

Another aspect of the Internet, which makes it quite appealing to those looking for health information, is the global nature of the Internet. People from all parts of the world can contribute to this sea of information as easily as can someone from North Carolina or Oregon. The rich diversity of the Internet brings some unique and interesting answers to many health questions. What makes this even more interesting is that many times, those who create these very interesting and unique Web pages place their E-mail address somewhere on the page so they can be contacted. Suppose you were reading someone's page on some type of alternative medicine for which you previously had no understanding. Perhaps after completing this information you still had some questions. Using the Internet and E-mail you can easily set up a dialogue with that person by sending them a letter and asking them your specific questions.

Never before has it been so simple to learn all you could ever want to know on just about any topic relating to health. At times it can be frustrating when you consider the enormous number of choices. With some patience and practice, however, you are no doubt going to enjoy the effectiveness and usefulness of the Internet at whatever level of researching you might find yourself.

part

1

Person-To-Person: Using E-mail

Electronic mail, or E-mail, is one of the most important applications of the Internet. E-mail is personal correspondence between individual users, and is the electronic equivalent to the familiar paper-based postal service.

How It Works

Every Internet Service Provider operates a post office 24 hours a day, 365 days per year to receive messages sent to its customers and to forward the mail they send to other people. Messages addressed to you are stored on the post office computer until you are ready to read them.

When you send an E-mail message to another person, you first transmit the message to your provider's post office which starts the message on its way to the post office at the recipient's service provider. Messages are usually passed between several post office computers on their way from one provider to another.

Personal Addresses on the Internet Each user on the Internet has a unique name. The name is made up of two parts: the user name and the domain name. The user name identifies the individual user, and the domain name identifies the Internet Service Provider.

For example, the E-mail address "psmith@uiuc.edu" is for a user named "P. Smith" at an organization (domain) called "uiuc.edu". The two pieces are always separated by '@'.

All domain names for organizations in the United States end with a three-letter abbreviation which specifies the type of organization. The common abbreviations are:

- .com   a company or business
- .edu   an educational institution
- .net   a commercial Internet service provider
- .org   an organization that is not a bus

Domain names from other parts of the world end with a two-letter abbreviation which specifies the country in which the organization is located. For example, "pat_smith@emwac.ed.ac.uk" is for a user named "Pat Smith" at an organization located in the United Kingdom.

Mail Programs

There are many different mail programs available, and they all provide similar functions and use similar terminology. We're going to give example from two popular mail programs: Netscape Mail and Microsoft Internet Mail.

Mail programs organize your messages in areas called *folders*. Typical folders are called **Inbox,** which holds the mail that has been sent to you, **Outbox** which holds mail you have written but not yet sent, and **Sent** which hold copies of messages you have sent to other people. You can also create your own folders as a way to save messages you have received in an organized fashion.

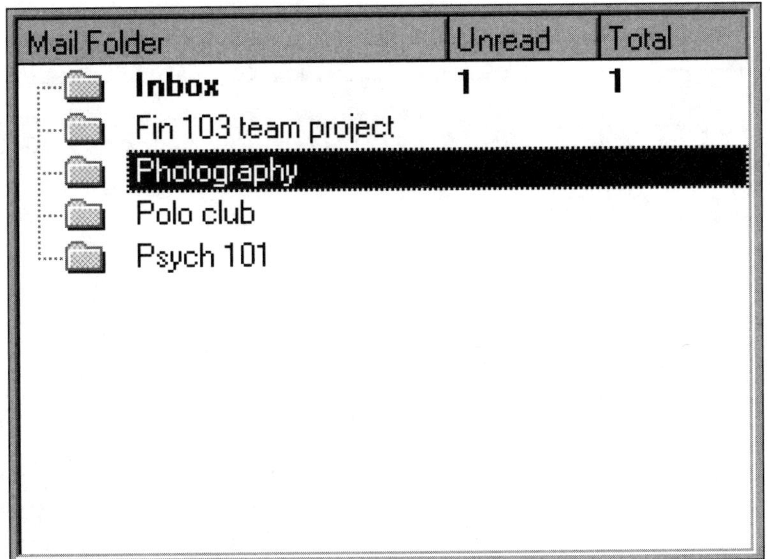

part

1

Using folders to organize messages you have received or sent can be a very convenient way to maintain a complete record of an E-mail "conversation."

Sending a Message

In this section we'll go step-by-step through the process of sending an E-mail message to another user. The steps are given for the Netscape Mail and Microsoft Internet Mail programs. If you are using a different mail program consult the program's documentation for complete instructions.

Using Netscape Mail

1. Click the To:Mail button in the toolbar or select the **New Mail Message** option from the **File** menu.

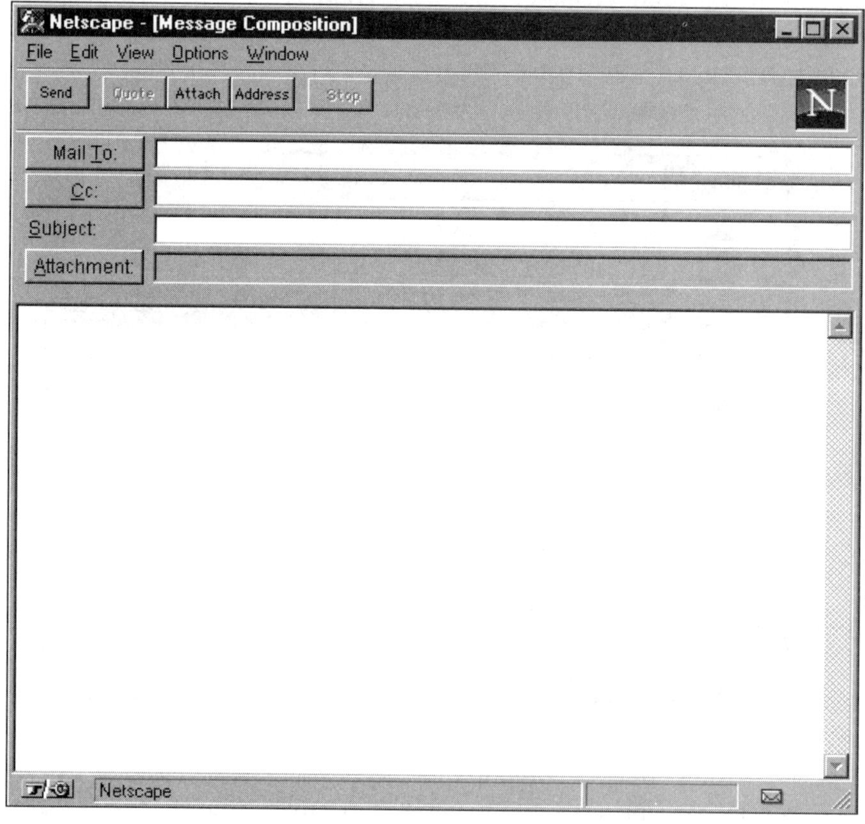

2. Type the recipient's E-mail address on the "Mail To:" line. If you want to send the same message to more than one person, put a semi-colon between the E-mail names. You can build up an electronic address book which can be accessed by clicking on the **Mail To:** button.

3. Press TAB to move to the "CC:" line. Type the address of people to whom you would like to send a copy of the message. Don't type anything here if you don't want to send copies or you have already listed everyone on the "To:" line.

4. Press TAB again and type a subject line for the message.

5. Press TAB again and type the body of your message. When you have finished writing the message, either click the **Send** button or choose the **Send Now** option from the **File** menu.

Using Microsoft Internet Mail

1. Click the **New Message** button in the toolbar or select the **New Message** option from the **Mail** menu.

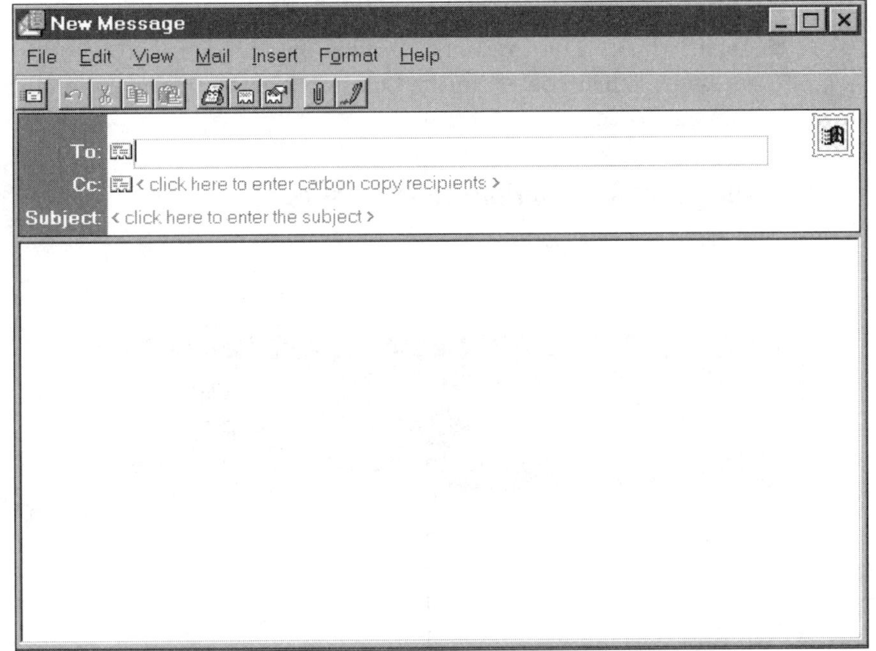

part

1

2. Type the recipient's E-mail address on the "To:" line. If you want to send the same message to more than one person, put a semicolon between the E-mail names. You can build up an electronic address book which can be accessed by clicking on the file card icon.

3. Press TAB to move to the "CC:" line. Type the address of people to whom you would like to send a copy of the message. Don't type anything here if you don't want to send copies or you have already listed everyone on the "To:" line.

4. Press TAB again and type a subject line for the message.

5. Press TAB again and type the body of your message. When you have finished writing the message, either click the send icon or choose the **Send Message** option from the **File** menu.

Your E-mail message starts it journey to the recipient's system as soon as you press the Send key. Once you send a message there is no way to get it back or stop it from reaching its destination.

Now practice sending a message by sending a message to yourself. Start your mail program and follow the steps listed above.

- Type your own E-mail address in the "Mail To:" or "To:" field.
- Leave the "CC:" field blank.
- Type "Test Message" on the "Subject line"
- Type "This is a test message. Did you get it?" for the body of the message. When you're finished use the "Send" option to send the message to yourself.

Reading and Responding to Messages

Using Netscape Mail

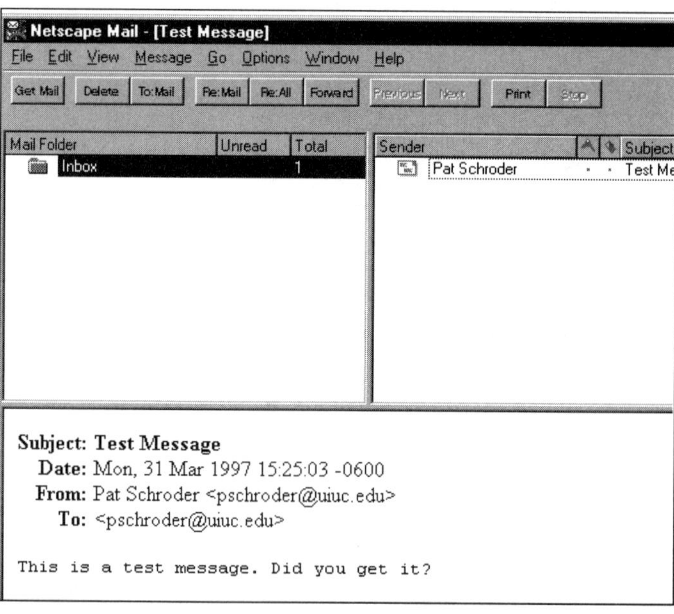

1. When you start Netscape Mail, the display shows a list of messages that have been sent to you. Messages that you have not yet read are listed in bold type.

   The "Sender" column shows who send the message, the "Subject" column displays the subject line, and the "Date" column shows the date on which the message was received.

2. The message you just sent to yourself should be listed in the window. Double-click the message line in the listing.

3. The message appears in the lower part of the window.

Using Microsoft Internet Mail

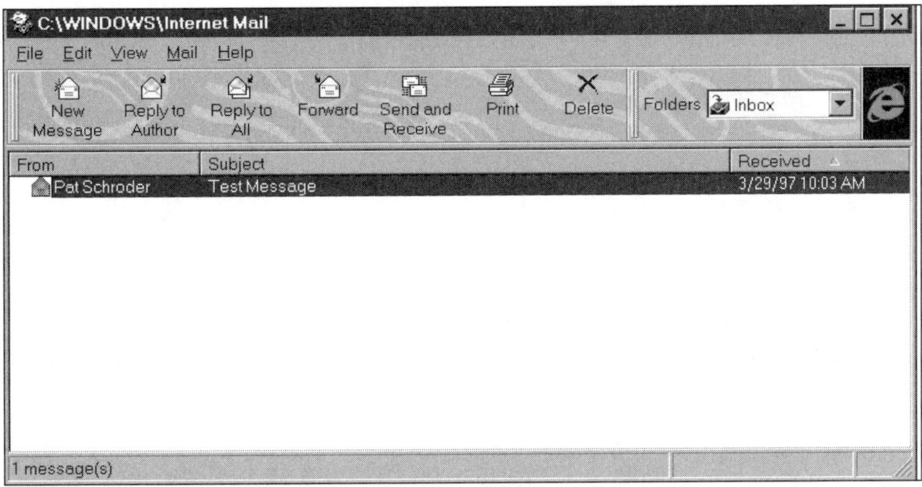

1. When you start Microsoft Internet Mail, the display shows a list of messages that have been sent to you. Messages that you have not yet read are listed in bold type.

   The "From" column shows who send the message, the "Subject" column displays the subject line, and the "Received" column shows the date on which the message was received.

2. The message you just sent to yourself should be listed in the window. Double-click the message line in the listing to open the mail reading window.

3. The message reader pops open and shows you the message.

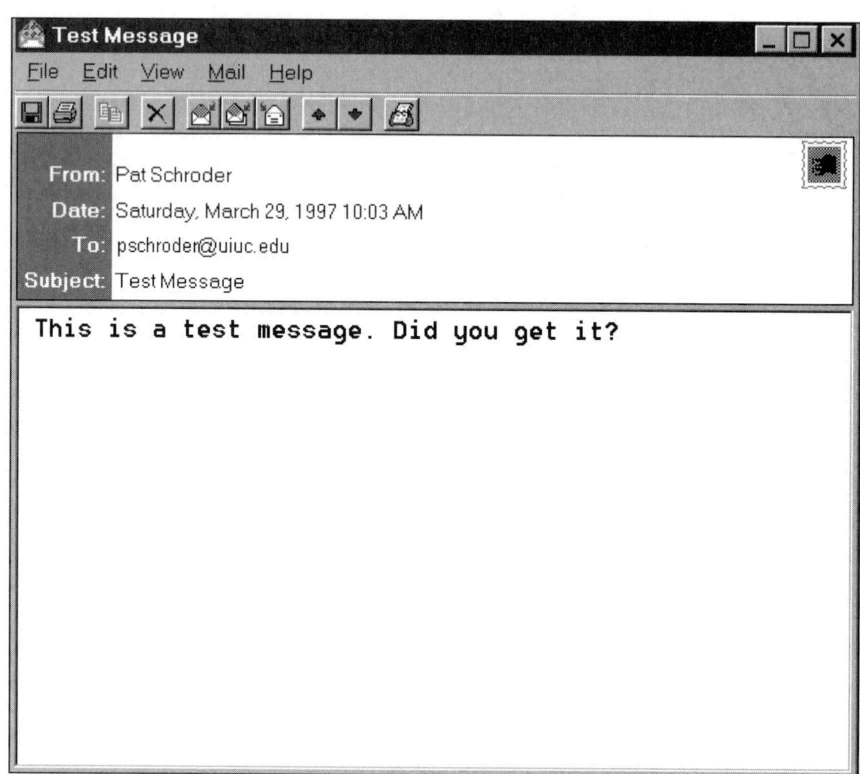

After you've read the message you can reply to it, then you can either delete it or file it in a folder for later reference. Using the reply feature of your mail reader is how you carry on an E-mail conversation. You receive a message that you reply to, then you receive a reply to your reply, you reply to that, and so on.

This kind of E-mail conversation may take place over a period of a few days or weeks; it's sometimes hard to keep the context of the conversation in mind when reading replies. Mail reader programs include a feature called Quoting that copies the message you are replying to and makes it part of your reply. When you use this feature you send back the original message along with your reply. This helps the person reading the reply remember the context of the message.

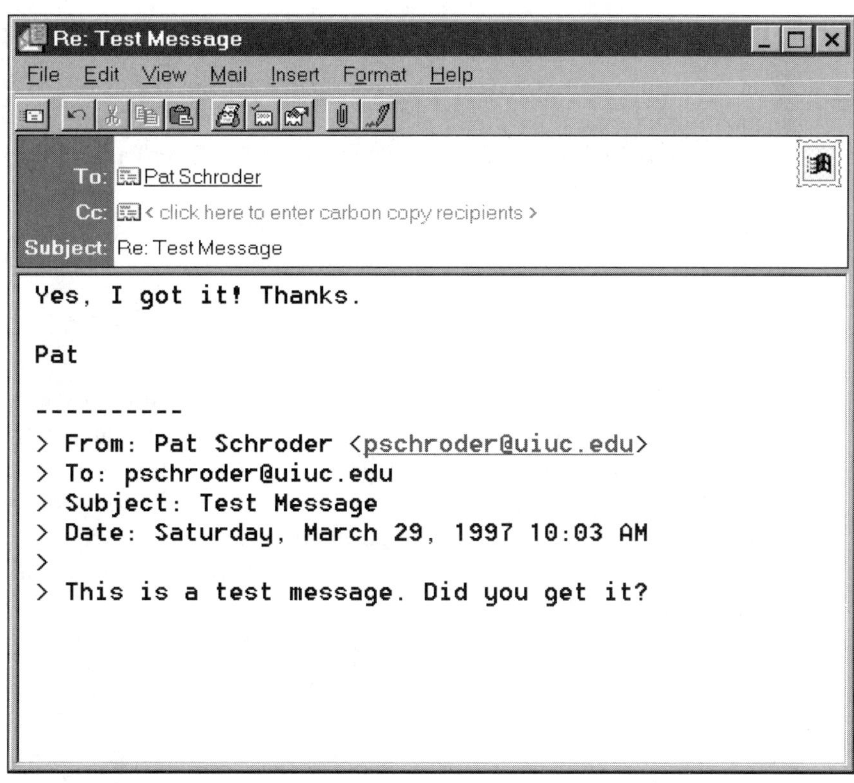

How to Locate Addresses

One major problem with the Internet is that there is no equivalent of the phone book. If you don't know someone's E-mail address there is no way to look them up in a directory. There are a few experimental directory assistance services in development, but so far they cover only a very small fraction of the millions of people who have E-mail addresses.

As you work with the Internet you will find many opportunities to compile an address book of E-mail addresses for future reference. Build up your own address book by watching for addresses on paper-based and electronic documents. Look for addresses on letterheads and other stationary. You should also copy the E-mail addresses from messages you receive. When you start surfing the Web (covered in a later chapter), you will have more opportunities to discover E-mail addresses.

To find E-mail addresses for health educators around the world go to: http://www.siu.edu/~kittle/HEDIR/Menu.html and click on one of the directories listed by job site, by name, or by state and country.

E-mail Etiquette

A set of etiquette rules have been developed over the years to make electronic interactions more pleasant and orderly. You should follow these rules of behavior, sometimes called "netiquette", when using E-mail.

Don't use all upper case. Using upper case letters to emphasize words in your messages is the E-mail equivalent of shouting. It's considered very bad manners to write messages in upper case.

Use emoticons and acronyms. The person reading your messages does not have the benefit of seeing your facial expressions and body language as with a face-to-face encounter. This is a very important limitation of E-mail, and you must always consider how your words might be interpreted. It's very hard for someone to know if you are kidding or are being very serious. *Emoticons* and acronyms have been developed over the years as a way of showing facial expressions or conveying feelings in the text of a message.

An emoticon is a set of characters that represent an emotion or facial expression. Common emoticons you may see in messages are:

: -)	smile
; -)	wink
: - n(	frown
<g>	grin
<vbg>	very big grin

An acronym is a form of shorthand. The letters of the acronym stand for an expression. Common acronyms in messages are:

AFAIK	as far as I know
IMO	in my opinion
IMHO	in my humble opinion
BTW	by the way
OTOH	on the other hand
CU	see you

Use emoticons and acronyms in your messages to help convey the subtle (or not-so-subtle) meanings behind your words. It may make a world of difference whether you write "Idiot!<g>" or "Idiot!" to the person reading your message.

Don't quote everything. Although quoting is a convenient way to maintain the context of a series of messages, messages become unreadable if you quote too much or quote a quote that includes a quote. Quote judiciously.

Keep your signature short. Some mail programs allow you to set up a *signature block*. This is a few lines of information that acts as your signature on a mail message. It's best not to put too much information in your signature block; your name and organizational affiliation are enough. You should not put your postal mailing address, phone number, fax number, Web site address, and favorite quote in your signature. Signatures should be very short, not longer than the messages they are attached to. Some people pay for E-mail services or have slow connections to the Internet, and this unnecessary information costs them time and money.

Be polite. Somewhere a researcher is studying the curious phenomenon that people will write things in an E-mail message that they would never say to someone's face. On the Internet, being intentionally rude and insulting is called *flaming* and has become a kind of sport for some people. You can unwittingly become the target of a flame attack by simply making a breach of netiquette in a public forum. If someone sends you an E-mail message calling you a "clueless newbie," you've been flamed.

Many people enjoy flaming newcomers to the Net. They will try to insult you because of your lack experience using the Net or the incorrect use of Internet terminology. Resist the temptation to reply to a flame attack. A flaming reply to a flame starts what is called a *flame war,* a kind of pointless Internet shouting match that can go on and on forever until one of the participants finally gives in at which point the opponent has "won" the war.

It's one thing to point out a mistake in someone's message, but do it in a polite way and back up your point with facts. A critical response should be more like a debate than a brawl. Don't just send a message saying, "Everyone knows such-and-such, and only a complete idiot and fool would think otherwise." Life's short. Lighten up.

part

1

On-Line Discussions: Newsgroups and Listservers

Newsgroups vs. E-mail

E-mail is a great person-to-person communication medium, but it's not very good for large group interaction. If the group consists of more than a few people, adding all the names to the "To:" or "CC:" list gets to be a tedious chore and it's hard to be sure that everyone sees the all of the replies. *Newsgroups* were developed to address this limitation.

A newsgroup is an electronic message board. The message board keeps track of several discussions simultaneously by organizing the messages and replies in groups called *threads.* A thread starts with the original message, or *post,* and includes all of the replies made by every participant in the discussion. You can follow the discussion by reading the thread from beginning to end. This makes it possible for several people to collaborate on a project or continue a discussion over a long period of time.

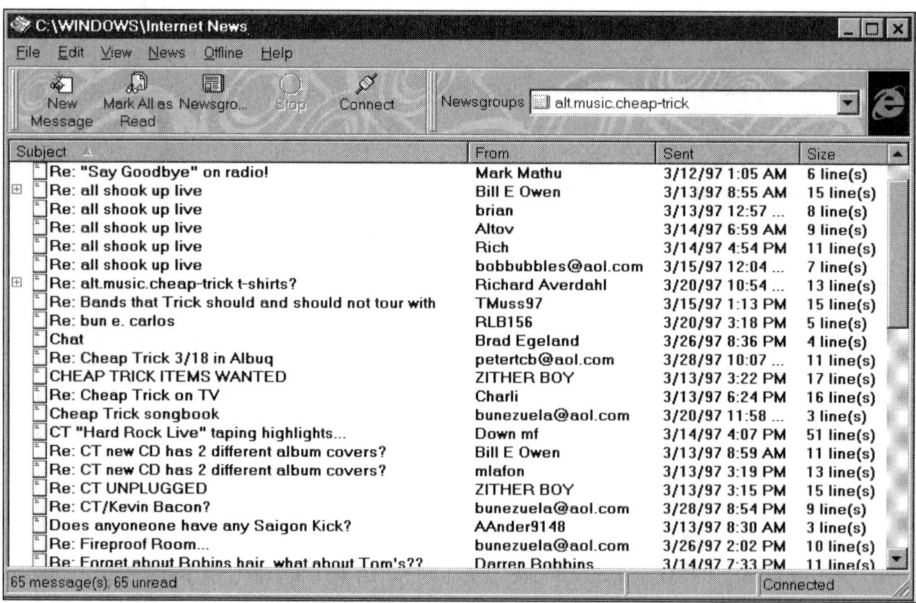

A program called a news reader is used to read newsgroups and follow the threads. News readers operate very much like E-mail programs,

but they also provide features that let you follow threads and keep track of your place in several continuing discussions. We'll be looking at the Netscape Navigator News Reader and the Microsoft Internet News programs for examples in this section. Other news readers offer similar services and work in much the same way.

Locating a Newsgroup

You can participate in tens of thousands of public and private newsgroups. You are usually invited to join a private newsgroup or find out about it because of your affiliation in an organization or participation in an activity. The discussion topics in a private newsgroup are likely to be very focused.

Your Internet Service Provider will carry as many as 20,000 public newsgroups in which you can participate. Just about every topic you can think of is covered, and a few that may shock and possibly offend you as well. When you hear stories on the news about all the smut and terrible things that are available on the Internet, the reporters are usually talking about newsgroups.

Newsgroups are organized in a hierarchy. There are a small number of main categories, each of which is broken down into subtopics, and further broken down into specific topics of interest. A sampling of the main categories you are likely to encounter includes:

comp	computer science and general computer-related topics
news	newsgroups pertaining to the operation of the Internet newsgroup system
rec	hobbies, recreational activities, and various arts
sci	scientific research, the applications of science and engineering, and some social sciences
soc	social issues
misc	anything that doesn't fit into the above categories
alt	"alternative" newsgroups, many unusual topics

The subtopics are, of course, different for each of the main categories. For example, within the "rec" category there is a subtopic "photo" for photographic-related discussions. This group of topics is called the "rec.photo" newsgroups. Notice that the main category is

part

1

named first, followed by a period, then the subtopic name. The specific newsgroup dedicated to the discussion of photographing people is called "rec.photo.people".

A newsgroup exists for nearly every aspect of health that you could imagine. About the only way to learn if a health related newsgroup might be interesting to you would be to check it out for yourself. Finding these newsgroups is not too difficult. You may type the words "health newsgroups" in your favorite search engine and see what you discover. After entering your request, the search engine will bring up many pages that list these health related newsgroups. One such page is titled "Newsgroups—The Good Health Web." Its URL (Internet address) is:

http://www.social.com/health/newsgroups.html

A long list of health related newsgroups appears. You may choose from any one of these that look particularly interesting. The titles of the newsgroups usually give you an idea of the focus for the newsgroup. Some of the newsgroups to choose from at this point include the following: alt.hypnosis, alt.meditation, misc.fitness, misc.health.alternative, misc.health.diabetes, misc.kids.health, rec.food.veg, sci.life-extension, sci.med.aids, sci.med.diseases.cancer, sci.med.nutrition, and talk.politics.medicine to name a few.

One of the best starting points for finding health related newsgroups is the Web site titled "Health A2Z." Its URL is:

http://www.HealthAtoZ.com/

Once there, click on the word "News Groups" and within a very short time you will find a limitless supply of information.

The list of newsgroups available to you is downloaded to your computer and kept up to date by the news group reader program. Specific instructions for browsing the newsgroup list depend on the particular newsgroup reader program.

Netscape Navigator News Reader

1. Select the **Show All Newsgroups** from the **Options** menu of Netscape Navigator. The list of available newsgroups is shown in the **News Servers** window. This window is organized like an outline. To locate a newsgroup you have to "expand" the levels of the outline. Click on the '+' sign next to an entry to see the subentries. Keep on clicking '+' signs until you get to the lowest level in the section you are interested in.

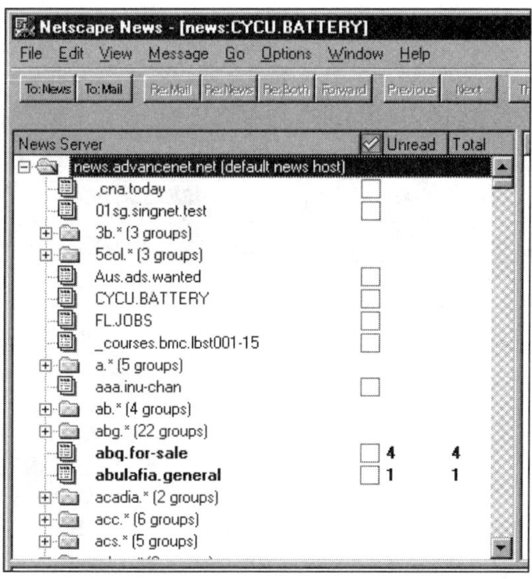

2. Click on the newsgroup name in the Newsgroups box. A list of messages appears in the window.

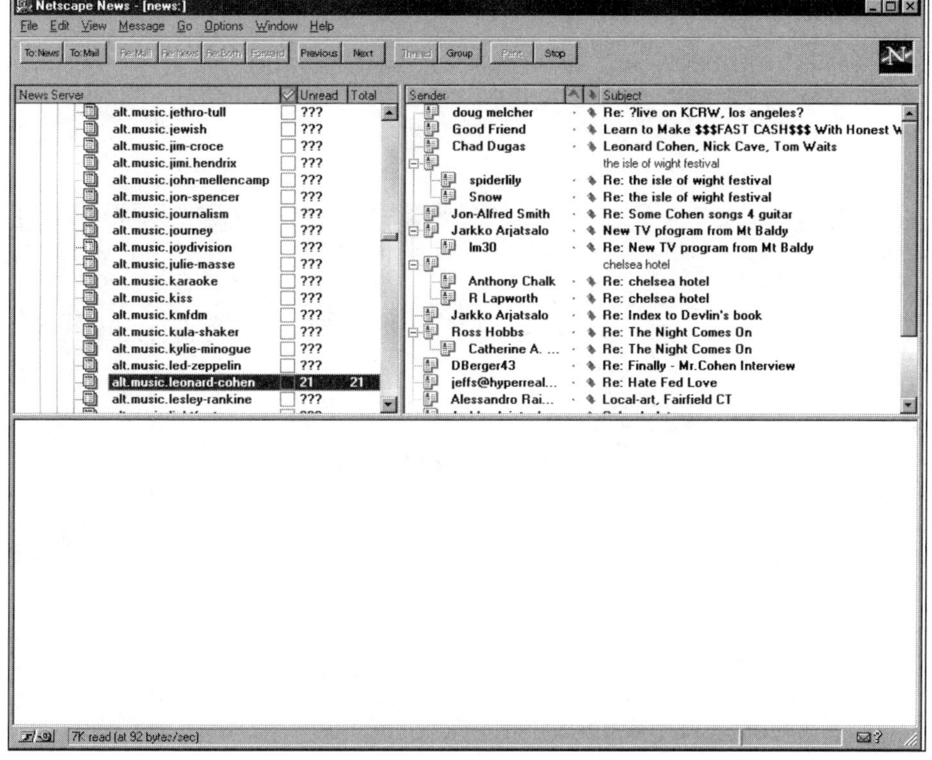

Microsoft Internet News

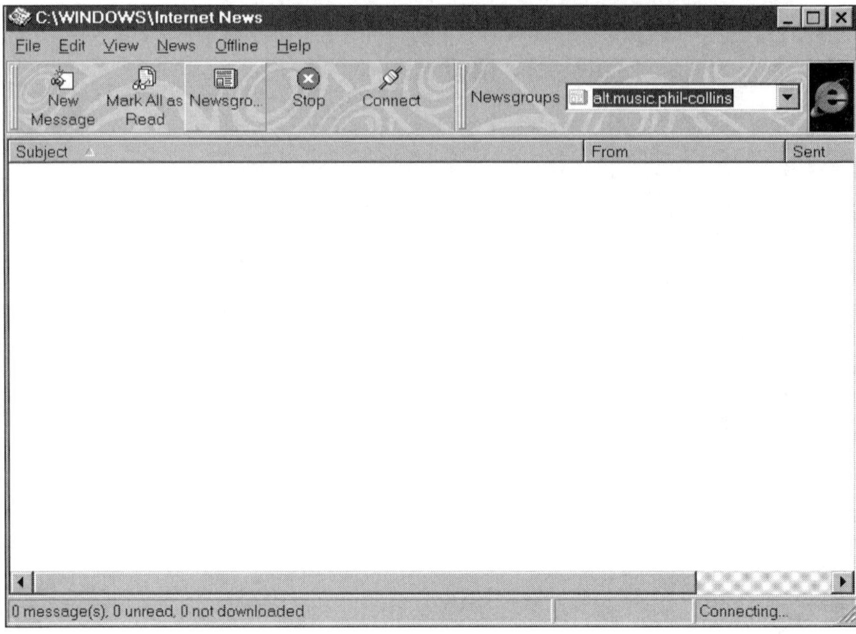

1. Click the **Newsgroups** button in the toolbar or select the **Newsgroups** option from the **News** menu.

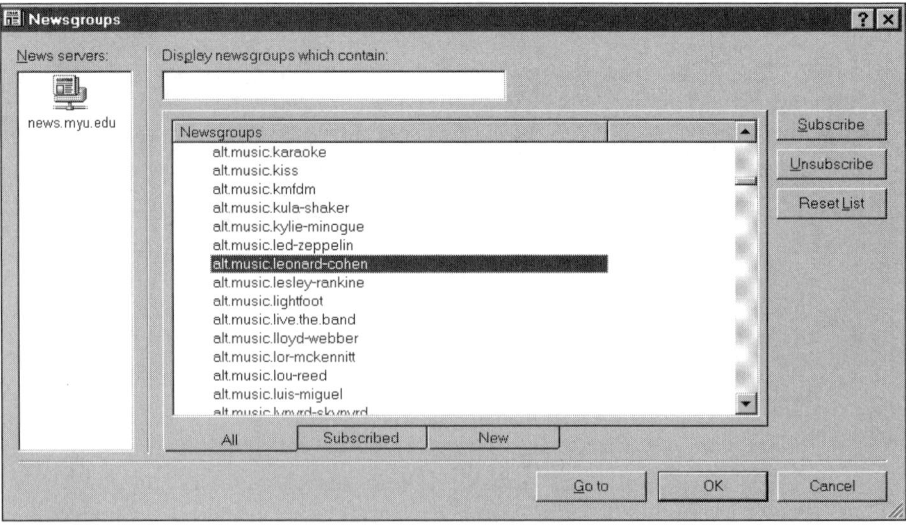

2. Click the **All** tab in the newsgroups window to display the entire list
   of newsgroups. You can browse the entire list of newsgroups by
   scrolling the list, or locate a newsgroup by typing a word in the
   "Display newsgroups which contain" box at the top of the page.

3. Click on the newsgroup name in the Newsgroups box and then
   click the **Go To** button to immediately see the messages for that
   newsgroup.

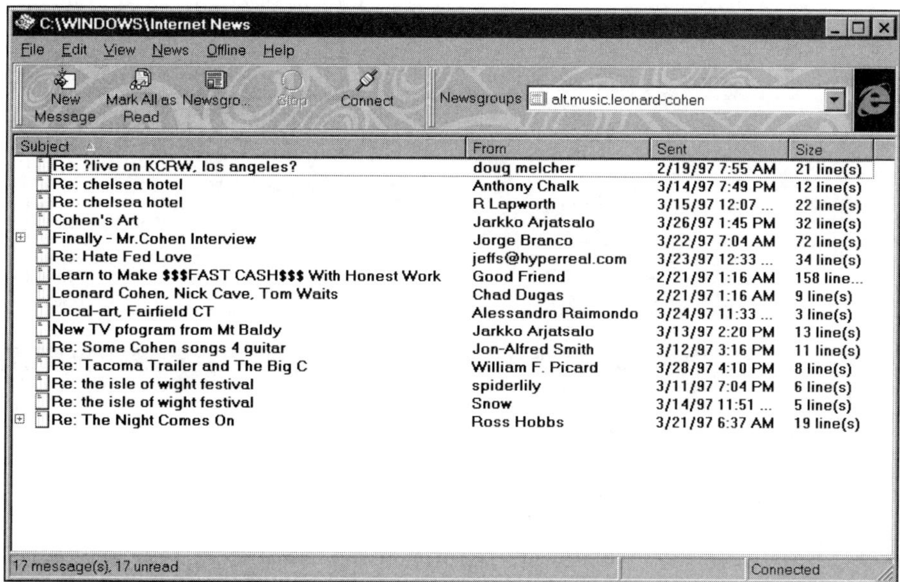

part

1

Reading Messages

Once you have selected a newsgroup the news reader program displays a
list of messages. The title of the message, name of the sender, and the
date on which the message was written are displayed. You will often see
"Re:" as the first part of the message title. That means "Regarding" and
indicates that the message is a reply to a previous message on the same
topic. Some news reader software automatically groups the messages by
topic. A series of messages on the same topic is called a *thread*.

Double click on the message title line to display the message. The
text of the message is displayed in a window.

Once you locate a newsgroup that you are interested in reading, you
have two choices. You can subscribe to the newsgroup and let your news
reader program keep track of which messages you have already seen, or

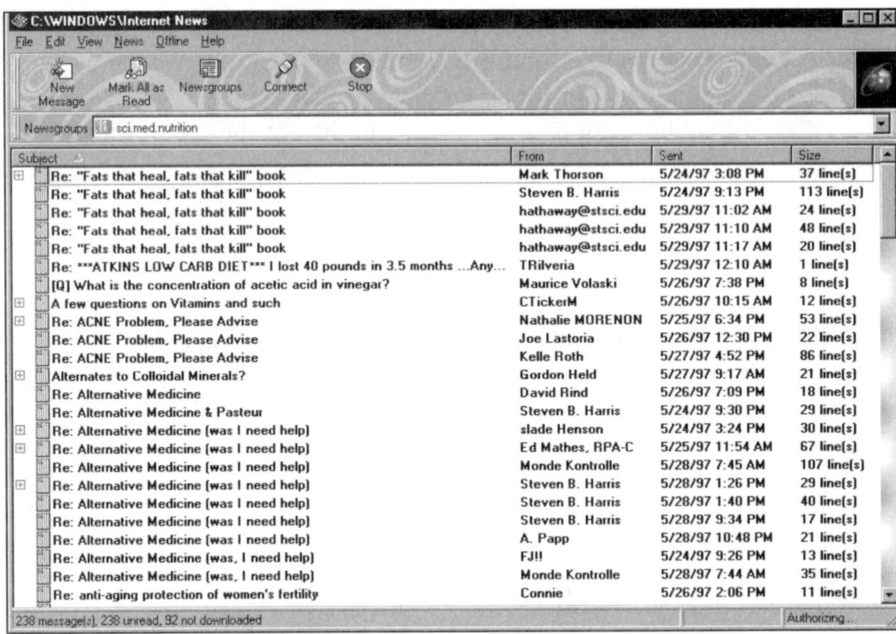

Subject	From	Sent	Size
Re: "Fats that heal, fats that kill" book	Mark Thorson	5/24/97 3:08 PM	37 line(s)
Re: "Fats that heal, fats that kill" book	Steven B. Harris	5/24/97 9:13 PM	113 line(s)
Re: "Fats that heal, fats that kill" book	hathaway@stsci.edu	5/29/97 11:02 AM	24 line(s)
Re: "Fats that heal, fats that kill" book	hathaway@stsci.edu	5/29/97 11:10 AM	48 line(s)
Re: "Fats that heal, fats that kill" book	hathaway@stsci.edu	5/29/97 11:17 AM	20 line(s)
Re: ***ATKINS LOW CARB DIET*** I lost 40 pounds in 3.5 months ...Any...	TRilveria	5/29/97 12:10 AM	1 line(s)
[Q] What is the concentration of acetic acid in vinegar?	Maurice Volaski	5/26/97 7:38 PM	8 line(s)
A few questions on Vitamins and such	CTickerM	5/26/97 10:15 AM	12 line(s)
Re: ACNE Problem, Please Advise	Nathalie MORENON	5/25/97 6:34 PM	53 line(s)
Re: ACNE Problem, Please Advise	Joe Lastoria	5/26/97 12:30 PM	22 line(s)
Re: ACNE Problem, Please Advise	Kelle Roth	5/27/97 4:52 PM	86 line(s)
Alternates to Colloidal Minerals?	Gordon Held	5/27/97 9:17 AM	21 line(s)
Re: Alternative Medicine	David Rind	5/26/97 7:09 PM	18 line(s)
Re: Alternative Medicine & Pasteur	Steven B. Harris	5/24/97 9:30 PM	29 line(s)
Re: Alternative Medicine (was I need help)	slade Henson	5/24/97 3:24 PM	30 line(s)
Re: Alternative Medicine (was I need help)	Ed Mathes, RPA-C	5/25/97 11:54 AM	67 line(s)
Re: Alternative Medicine (was I need help)	Monde Kontrolle	5/28/97 7:45 AM	107 line(s)
Re: Alternative Medicine (was I need help)	Steven B. Harris	5/28/97 1:26 PM	29 line(s)
Re: Alternative Medicine (was I need help)	Steven B. Harris	5/28/97 1:40 PM	40 line(s)
Re: Alternative Medicine (was I need help)	Steven B. Harris	5/28/97 9:34 PM	17 line(s)
Re: Alternative Medicine (was I need help)	A. Papp	5/28/97 10:48 PM	21 line(s)
Re: Alternative Medicine (was, I need help)	FJ!!	5/24/97 9:26 PM	13 line(s)
Re: Alternative Medicine (was, I need help)	Monde Kontrolle	5/28/97 7:44 AM	35 line(s)
Re: anti-aging protection of women's fertility	Connie	5/26/97 2:06 PM	11 line(s)

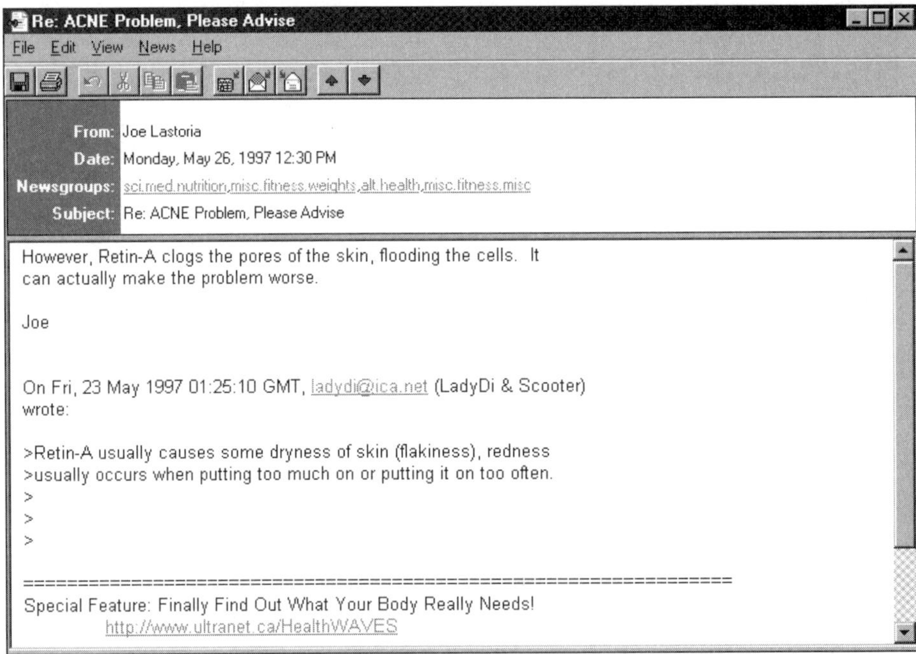

From: Joe Lastoria

Date: Monday, May 26, 1997 12:30 PM

Newsgroups: sci.med.nutrition,misc.fitness.weights,alt.health,misc.fitness.misc

Subject: Re: ACNE Problem, Please Advise

However, Retin-A clogs the pores of the skin, flooding the cells. It
can actually make the problem worse.

Joe

On Fri, 23 May 1997 01:25:10 GMT, ladydi@ica.net (LadyDi & Scooter)
wrote:

>Retin-A usually causes some dryness of skin (flakiness), redness
>usually occurs when putting too much on or putting it on too often.
>
>
>

===
Special Feature: Finally Find Out What Your Body Really Needs!
          http://www.ultranet.ca/HealthWAVES

you can just drop in from time to time and notice whether there are new messages. Subscribing doesn't cost you anything and is the most convenient option of you are going to be a frequent reader of a particular newsgroup.

Subscribing is easy. If you use Microsoft Internet News, simply click the **Subscribe** button after selecting the newsgroup in the newsgroup window. If you use Netscape Navigator News Reader, click the checkbox next to the newsgroup name in the **News Server** window.

Posting and Responding to Messages

It's always a good idea to follow a newsgroup for a while before posting messages yourself. Reading messages and never posting is called *lurking*. Lurk for a few days so you will know what type of messages and topics are appropriate for the list.

Replies to messages can be posted to the newsgroup for all participants to see, or you can send a personal reply to the message author by E-mail.

You can also start a new thread by posting your own message to the newsgroup. This is very similar to sending E-mail, but instead of addressing the message to one person you post it to the list for all participants to see.

Responsible Participation: Newsgroup Etiquette

All the etiquette rules that apply to E-mail apply to newsgroups as well. Since messages in newsgroups may be read by thousands of people, however, there are a few additional rules you should keep in mind.

Keep it short. Keep your messages to newsgroups short and to the point. Many people have to pay for access to the Internet and the extra time needed to download long or off-topic messages costs them money.

Don't believe everything you read. There's no control over what's posted in most newsgroups, so you're likely to find all types of information. Some of it is profane and inflammatory, and some of it is just plain wrong. If you are easily offended you should be careful which newsgroups you read. Be careful about believing anything you read in a newsgroup, especially if it's some type of rumor or gossip. Some people make a sport out of posting outlandish rumors, or intentionally post factually incorrect information. When you read a message in a newsgroup, pay attention to the name of the author. Pretty soon you will figure out who is reliable and who isn't. Newsgroups are a great source of information and peer support, but don't believe everything you read. If you have children, you may want to restrict their access to newsgroups. Many contain language and content that's not appropriate for children.

part

1

Be tolerant. Newsgroups are read by people all over the world, many of whom do not use English as their native language. Never flame or correct anyone's spelling or grammar, and be very tolerant of misused phrases or "broken English."

Don't send spam. Easy access to the Internet has spawned a new breed of junk mail known as *spam*. Spam is a message promising a new way to loose weight, get rich quick, or something similar. Some of these messages are chain letters, others are outright scams and hoaxes. A spam message is never about the topic of the newsgroup to which it has been posted. Don't respond to spam messages, and do not post off-topic messages like that yourself!

Keep cross posting to a minimum. *Cross posting* means that a message will be sent to more than one newsgroup simultaneously. This can be compared to running from room to room at a party and carrying on the same conversation with different groups of people. Since many people who read newsgroups follow many groups on similar topics, cross posted messages almost always reach the same audience anyway. It is very annoying to see similar, but slightly different threads in different newsgroups. Never post a message to more than two or three newsgroups, and be sure you have a very good reason for doing so.

Group Discussion via E-mail (Listservers)

Setting up a newsgroup is not an easy process, so many special interest groups use a variation of E-mail to pass messages to all of the group members. A *listserver* is a program that automatically distributes messages to all the members of the list. Once you join a list, the listserver will send you all messages via standard E-mail. You can reply to a message or start a new discussion by sending an E-mail message to the listserver program instead of sending copies of a message to each member individually.

Listservers are convenient because they insure that all members of the list see all the posted messages, including all replies between members. Some listserver programs will accumulate and combine messages into a *digest*. A digest allows the listserver to send one large message to each member on a periodic basis rather than sending many small messages all the time. For very active lists it's easier for the members and more efficient for the Internet for list members to use the digest form.

Finding a Mailing List

There are thousands of mailing lists, so how do you find lists on your favorite topics? There are several ways. First, you will see references to lists as you read newsgroups and carry on discussions with colleagues. Second, there are some resources on the World Wide Web that you can search by topic to find the names of mailing lists that may be of interest. And third, you can obtain lists of lists via E-mail.

"Health A2Z"—**http://www.HealthAtoZ.com/**— is one of the best "first stops" to locate a mailing list that you may find interesting. It includes an enormous directory of mailing lists that are health related including such topic areas as: Allied Health, Consumer Health, Drug Use and Abuse, Diseases and Conditions, Fitness and Exercise, Men's Health, Women's Health, and Public Health & Prevention to name only a few.

Participating in Discussions

To participate in a mailing list discussion you must subscribe to or join the list. Each list has two addresses, the subscription or listserver address, and the submissions address. Use the listserver address to join or quit the list; use the submissions address to send a message to members of the mailing list.

Listserver addresses almost always start with "listserv," "listproc," or "majordomo."

For example, the list dedicated to the discussion of holistic health and holistic medicine is called HOLISTIC-L and is managed by the listserver located at LISTSERV@SIU.EDU. Submissions to the list are mailed to: HOLISTIC-L@SIU.EDU

Whenever you want to manage your subscription by joining or quitting the list, you send an E-mail message to the listserver. When you want to write a message that will be sent to the other subscribers of the list you send an E-mail message to the submission address.

For example, the list dedicated to writers of poetry is called POETRY-W and is managed by the listserver located at "listserv@psuvm.psu.edu." Submissions to the list are mailed to "POETRY-W@psuvm.psu.edu." Whenever you want to manage your subscription by joining or quitting the list, you send an E-mail message to the listserver. When you want to write a message that will be sent to the other subscribers of the list you send an E-mail message to the submission address.

part

1

Specific instructions for subscribing depend on how the list was set up, but the normal procedure to subscribe to a list is:

1. Send an E-mail message to the listserver by putting the listserver's address on the "To:" line of the message. Do not use the submission address for the list!

2. Leave the subject line of the message blank. If your E-mail program will not let you send a message with a blank subject, use "subscribe" on the subject line.

3. In the body of the message type "subscribe *listname*" where you will substitute the name of the list for *listname.*

In a short time you will receive E-mail telling you that your subscription request has been accepted, or you will get back an error message saying that the listserver did not understand your subscription request. If you get an error message the best thing to do is to send a one-line message to the listserver address that simply says "help." This will usually get you an E-mail message with all the details on how to subscribe to a list on that listserver.

Save the notice the listserver sends when you are finally enrolled as a subscriber. This notice will contain useful information such as how to get off the list, whether or not a digest form is available and how to receive it, how to get back issues, and so on.

After your subscription has been accepted the listserver will start forwarding to you, via E-mail, all messages submitted to the list. You can participate in the discussion by sending an E-mail message to the submission address. Remember that your message will be forwarded to many people, so follow the rules of netiquette.

If you subscribe to an active list, be sure to read your E-mail frequently. Some lists generate hundreds of messages a week, and your mailbox will fill up quickly if you don't log on frequently to clean it up. You may want to investigate the use of "mail filtering rules" or "inbox assistant" features of your mail reader program to automatically sort messages into folders as they arrive in your mailbox. Check the **Help** section of your mail program for the details of using these features.

Some mailing lists have several thousand people who read and contribute to the lists. With that many people, the possibility of a very large number of daily letters in your mailbox is high. At first this might seem exciting to receive that much E-mail. If you subscribe to more than one of these mailing lists, you will be receiving an even larger number of

E-mail letters, each day. It is wise to determine the amount of time you have to read your E-mail. Follow the feel of the list for a month or two and see if you want to remain subscribed to that list.

Additionally, to avoid filling your mailbox, it is useful to set your browser to check your mailbox from time to time. Usually one check every hour or two is sufficient.

The Internet as a Library: Using the Web for Research

The fastest and most popular part of the Internet is the World Wide Web. The Web consists of hundreds of thousands of computers, each publishing information you can use. Some of the information is very useful, such as on-line library card catalogs, information from organizations, and subject-specific information you can't find anywhere else. You'll also find loads of useless, tasteless, and incorrect information and propaganda. On the Web, everyone and anyone can be a publisher.

The Web got its name because each site usually contains *links* to other sites the publisher thinks are related. Since each site has links to other sites, a kind of Web is formed. This is the great power of the Web. Once you find a site that contains information you find useful, you can follow the links to other sites you think may be interesting then continue with your research. This is like using the bibliography of one book to find other books, only much faster.

Structure of the Web: Making Order out of Chaos

Unfortunately, there's no overall organization for Web sites—no classification system or central catalog. Anyone can publish information on the Web. The result can be compared to a library without a book numbering system or card catalog. You must roam around until you happen to find what you are looking for.

The trick to finding information on the Web is to keep a short of list of sites that specialize in cataloging information from other Web sites, keep your own personal list of favorite Web sites, and learn to use at least one of the many *search engines* that will scan the Internet looking for Web sites that contain keywords or phrases that you specify.

part

1

Navigating the Web

Navigating the Web requires a program called a *browser*. The browser keeps track of where you are on the Web and displays the information sent to your computer by the Web site. Using the Web is an interactive process. Information is sent to you as you request it.

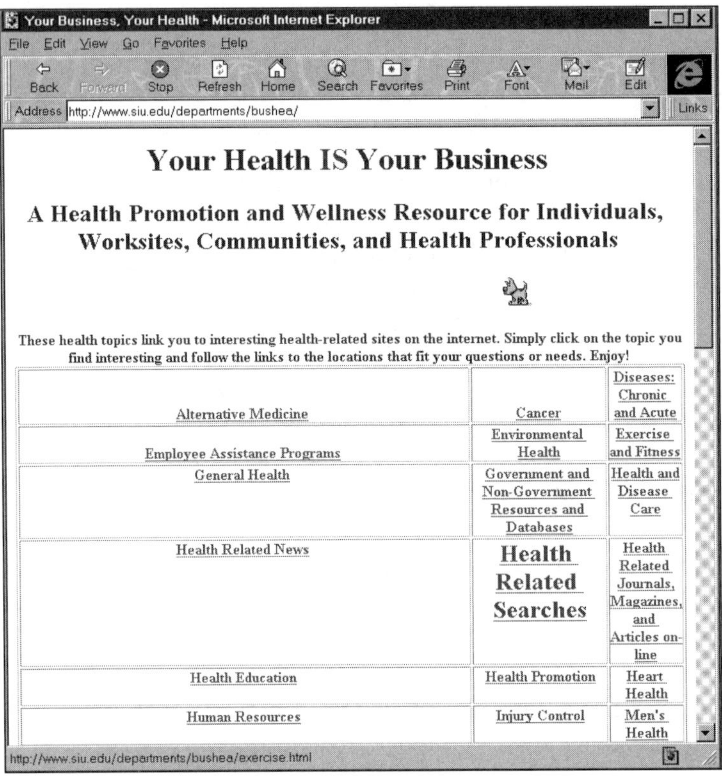

Information on the Web is independent of the type of computer you are using. It doesn't matter if you are using a Macintosh or PC-compatible. To view information on any site, all you need is a browser for your specific computer.

There are several browsers on the market, but the two most popular are Netscape Navigator and Microsoft Internet Explorer. We'll show examples from both of those browsers in this section.

All browsers offer similar basic functions. The basic functions are:

- Site Name Selection: Go to a specific Web site
- HyperText Link: Move to a new site when an on-screen link is selected

- **Back** button: Back up to the previous site
- **Forward** button: Move forward to return to the site you just moved back from
- **Home** button: Go to your home or starting page
- **Print** button: Print the current page
- **Refresh** button: Refresh the current display

Uniform Resource Locators (URLs) Each site on the Web has an address called a Uniform Resource Locator, or *URL*. The URL always starts with the letters "http://". The colon and two slash characters are required. These letters tell the Web browser that the address you are about to give is for a Web site. Next comes the name of the site itself. Most, but not all, Web sites use the letters "www" as the first part of their name. For example, Microsoft's Web site's address is "http://www.microsoft.com" and the Web site for the University of Illinois in Urbana-Champaign is at "http://www.uiuc.edu".

part

1

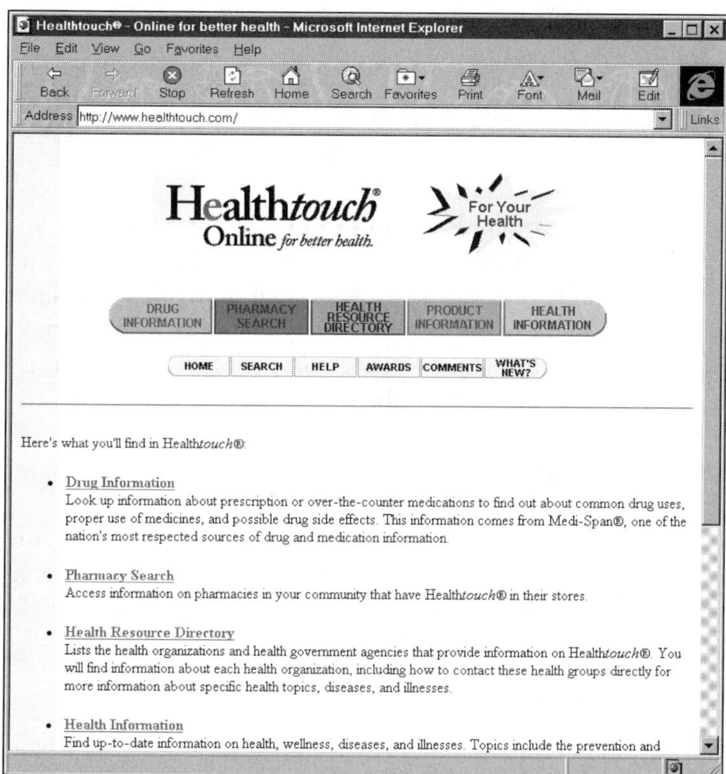

Health Related URL with an obvious name: http://www.health touch.com/

You can often guess the Web site address for large companies by typing "http://www.*name*.com", putting the company name or abbreviation in place of *name.*

The toolbar at the top of your browser window contains a place for you to type the address of the Web site you want to see. In Netscape Navigator it's labeled "Go to:" and in Microsoft Internet Explorer it's labeled "Address:". Both programs expect you to type the URL in exactly the same format. The URL for the site and page you are currently viewing will be displayed in this area as you navigate your way around the Web.

When you start your browser it will always take you to the same starting point or *home page.* The home page will usually contain links to other sites and so enables you to begin your Web exploration from a known point.

Browser Basics The actual display of information from a Web site depends on the computer you have, the browser you are using, and the features programmed into the Web page by the publisher. Some pages are only text; others are complex multimedia affairs that incorporate sound and video. Your browser will do its best to display the information from a site on your computer even if you do not have all the options required. For example, if your computer does not have sound capability, the browser will not try to play audio tracks from Web sites that incorporate them.

HyperText When you look at a page in the browser window you'll see some highlighted words and phrases. The highlight is usually a different color than the main text as well as an underline. Highlighted phrases are the *links* to other pages on the Web. Click your mouse on a highlighted phrase and the browser will jump you to the appropriate location. This type of text with embedded links to related details is called *hypertext.*

A health related page with downloadable file links can be found at: ftp://mirrors.aol.com/pub/info-mac/_Education

Some links are to programs or data files that can be downloaded to your computer. When you click on one of these links you will see a box asking for permission to download the file. Choose the "Save File" button on the dialog and the file will be sent to your computer.

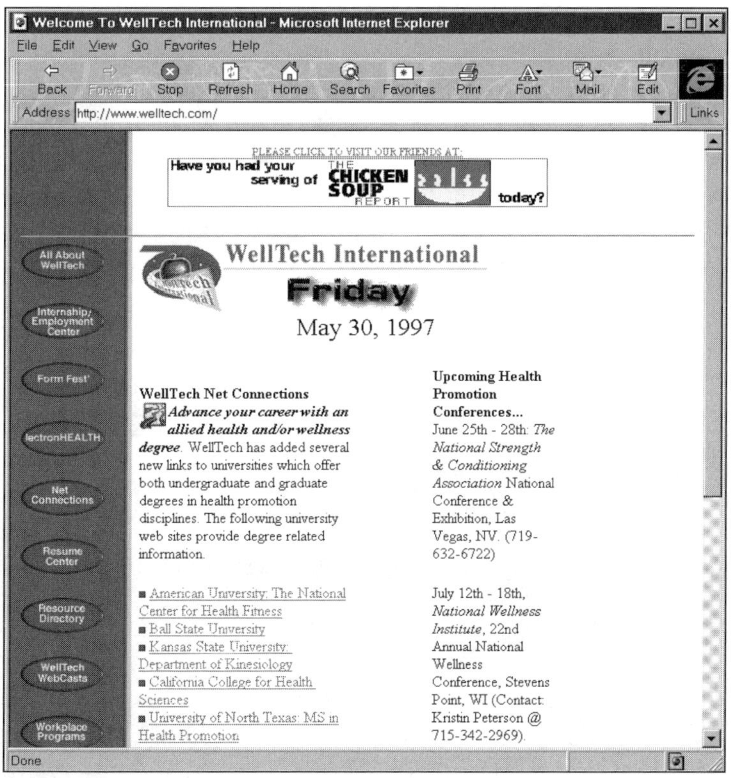

A health related page with many text links can be found at: http://www.welltech.com/

AUTHOR: No response from website. Please advise.

A health related page with downloadable file links can be found at:
ftp://mirrors.aol.com/pub/info-mac/_Education

Image Maps As the design of Web pages became more sophisticated, it was soon discovered that text links were inconvenient for many applications. For example, a site with weather information on the continental US would be easier to navigate if the user clicked a point on a map instead of choosing a location from a long list of text links. With this simple idea the *image map* was born.

Many sites incorporate image maps for quick navigation. You will see many uses of image maps as you navigate the Web. As you move your mouse cursor over a graphic, the pointer will change to indicate that the graphic is a clickable image map.

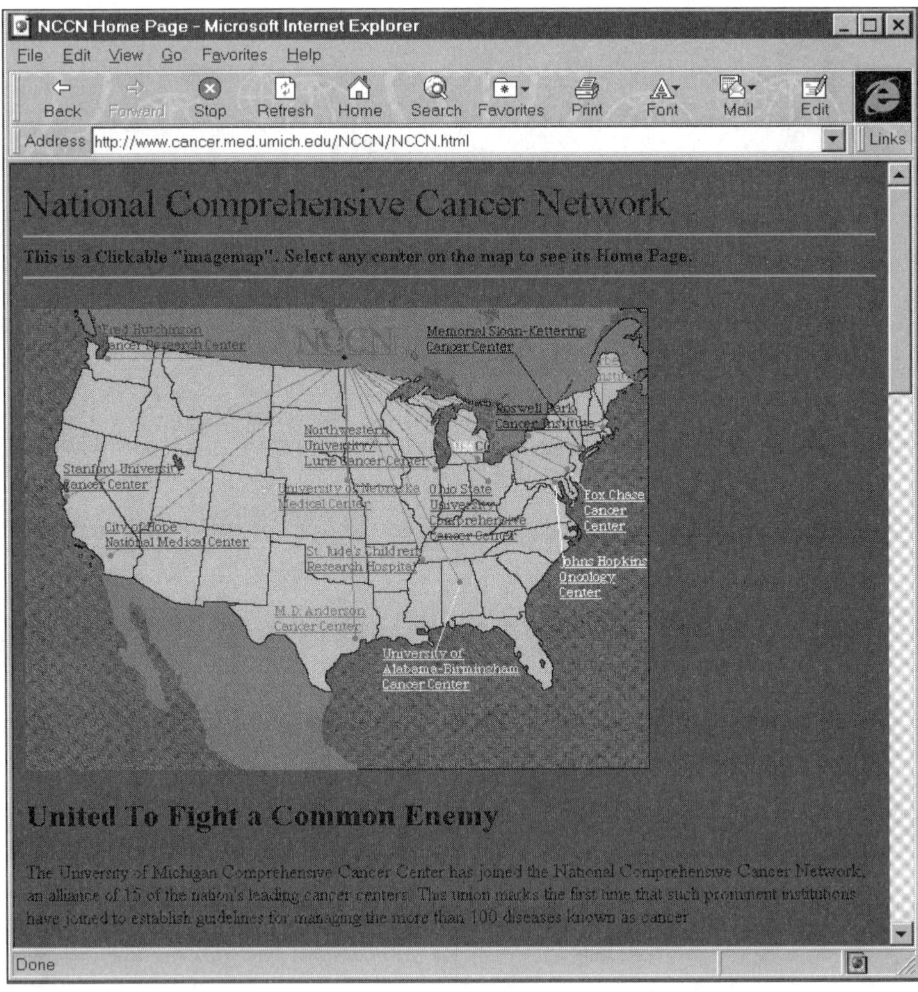

Using Bookmarks and History Files All browsers allow you to set electronic bookmarks, which enable you to return to a Web page without going through other links. This is useful when you find a site you think would be interesting to explore when you have more time, or when you finally find what you're looking for after following dozens of links.

Netscape Navigator files bookmarks under the **Bookmark** menu and Microsoft Internet Explorer files them in the **Favorites** menu, but they work the same way. When you reach a site you want to bookmark:

1. Select the **Add Bookmark** option from the **Bookmark** menu in Navigator, or the **Add to Favorites** option from the **Favorites** menu in Internet Explorer.

2. Navigator immediately adds the site name to the **Bookmark** menu. Internet Explorer pops up a window that allows you to edit the name of the site and to organize your bookmarked favorites in folders.

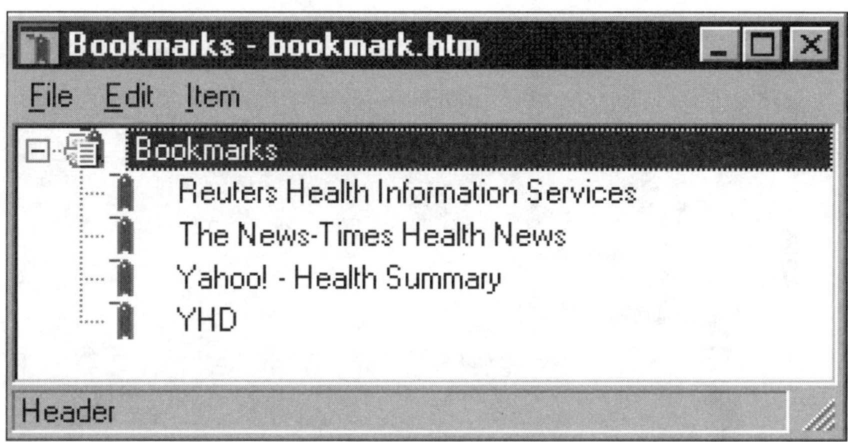

To return to a bookmarked site, pull down the **Bookmark** menu in Navigator or the **Favorites** menu in Internet Explorer and click on the name of the bookmark.

Your browser is also recording the name of every Web site you visit as you surf around the Net. This is called a *history file* and lets you return to any site you have visited recently. Netscape Navigator gives you access to the history file from the **History** option in the **Window** menu. Microsoft Internet Explorer shows the history file via the **Open History Folder** option in the **Go** menu.

Customizing the Browser

You will find browsing the Web more convenient if you modify the browser to suite your personal taste and needs. The most common customizations are:

- Choosing fonts and colors
- Turning graphics, audio, and video on and off for faster browsing
- Choosing a start page

Netscape Navigator To customize Netscape Navigator, select **General Preferences** from the **Options** menu. The sections available include Appearance, Fonts, Colors, Images, Apps, Helpers, and Language.

Appearance
The Appearance page allows you to make modifications by using fonts, colors, and images.

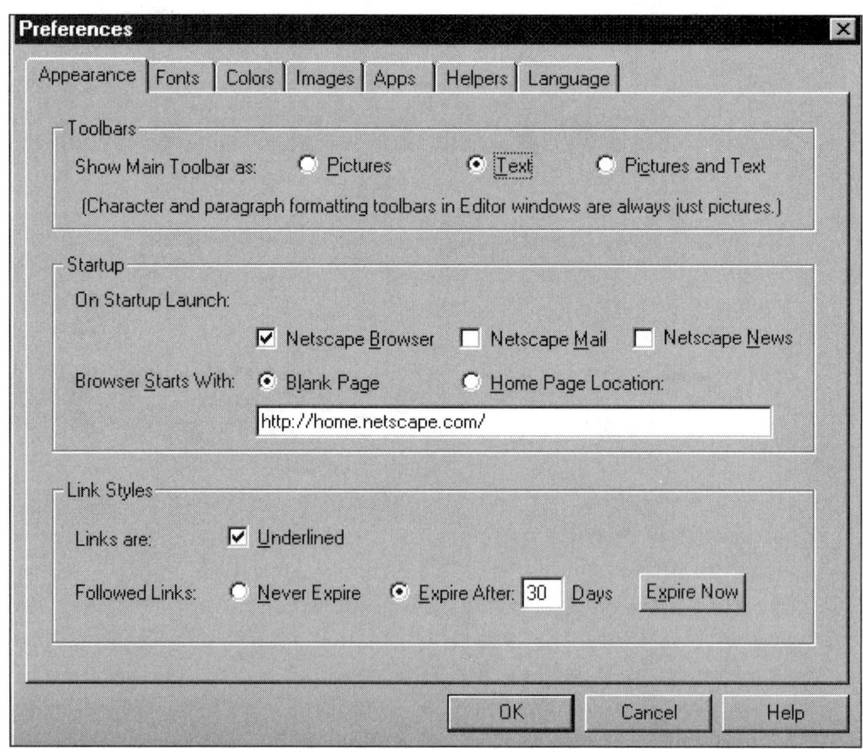

Toolbars Changes the way the toolbar in the main Netscape Navigator window is displayed. If you have a small monitor you may want to select "Text" style to reduce the space taken by the Toolbar.

Startup Specifies whether Netscape Navigator will show the Web browser, mail reader, or news reader when it first starts. You can also specify a Web page to act as a jumping-off point every time you start the browser. This is useful if you always want to begin with a search engine or the Web page from a specific organization.

Link Styles These options affect the way links are displayed and how long history files are kept. Leave these options at their default settings until you get more experience with Netscape Navigator. Then you can check the *Help* section for more detailed information on their use.

Fonts

The *Fonts* page lets you change the basic font Netscape Navigator uses to display the text on Web pages. There are two fonts you can set. The proportional font is used for all "normal" text. You may want to

part
1

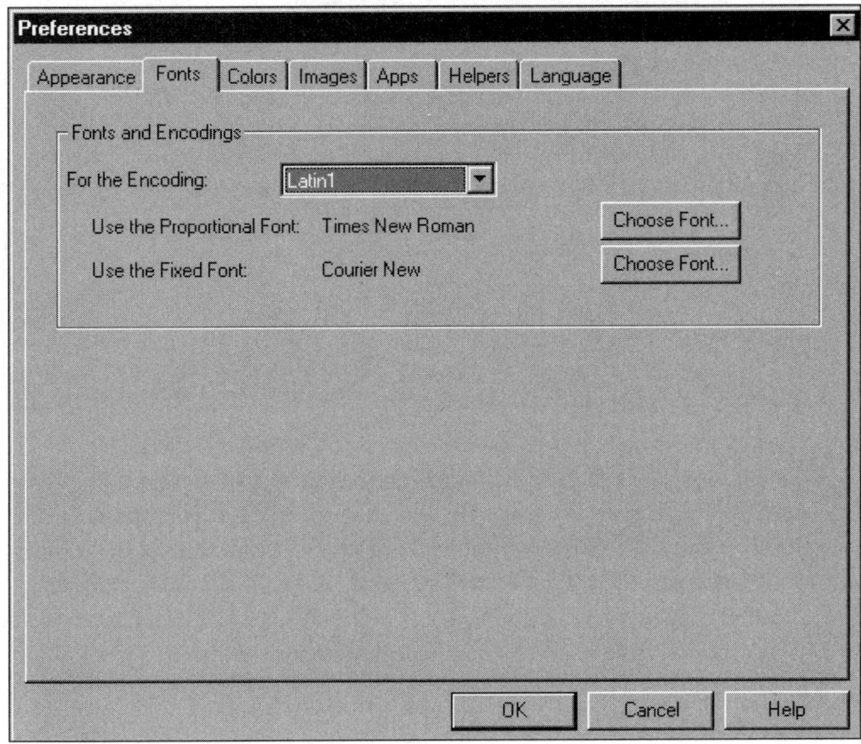

decrease the size of this font so the browser can show more of the page in the window, or you may prefer to increase the size of the font to make the pages easier to read. The fixed font is used for some tabular material, and does not have as great an effect on the readability of the display.

Do not change the *Encoding* selection unless you routinely visit non-English language sites and have a specific reason to make the change.

Colors

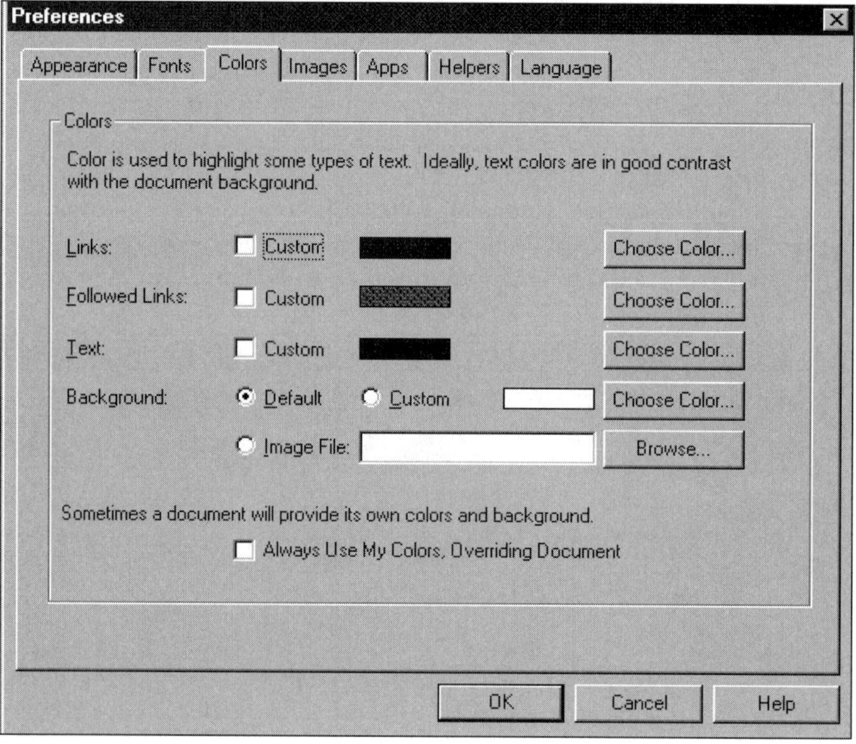

The Color settings are the default values used by Netscape Navigator if the Web publisher does not use specific colors. *Links* is the color of a link on the Web page. *Followed Links* is for links that point to sites you have seen recently. *Text* is the standard text color, and *Background* is the standard page background color. The default values are probably acceptable unless you discern certain colors better than others.

Images

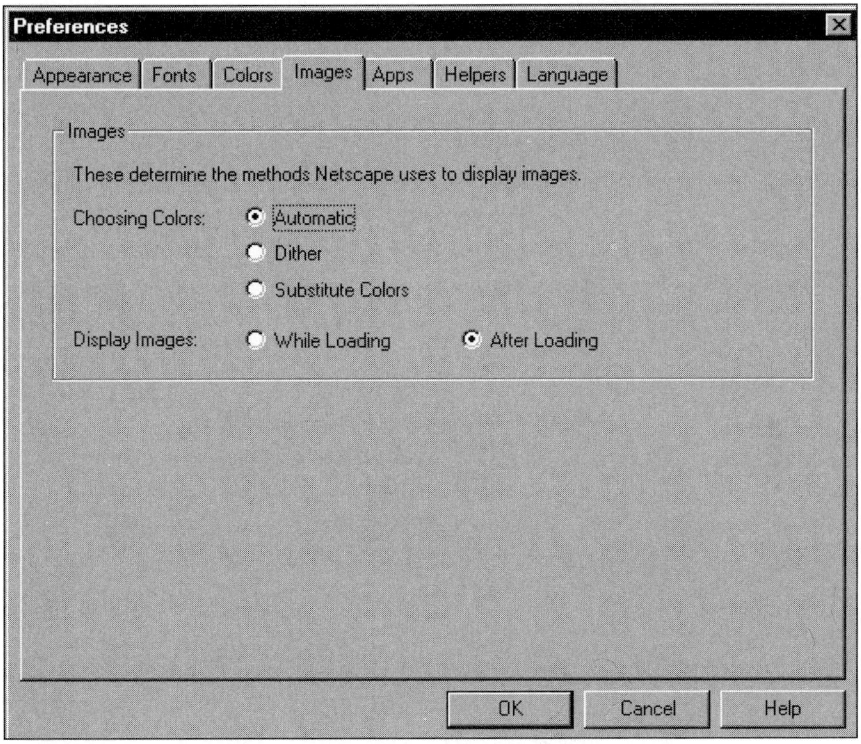

This page lets you specify how Netscape Navigator will handle pictures displayed on Web pages. Leave the Color setting set to *Automatic.* If you have a modem on your computer and connect to the Web over a telephone line, you may find Web browsing faster if you change the *Display Images* selection to "After loading." This tells Netscape Navigator to load and display all text on the page, then the pictures. This setting can save you time. After reading some or all of the text while the graphics load, you may decide the site is not useful and go on to another without waiting for the pictures. Try the setting both ways to see which you like best.

Apps, Helpers, and Language

Do not make any changes to the settings on the *Apps, Helpers,* or *Language* pages unless you have very specific reasons for doing so, and have the assistance of an experienced user.

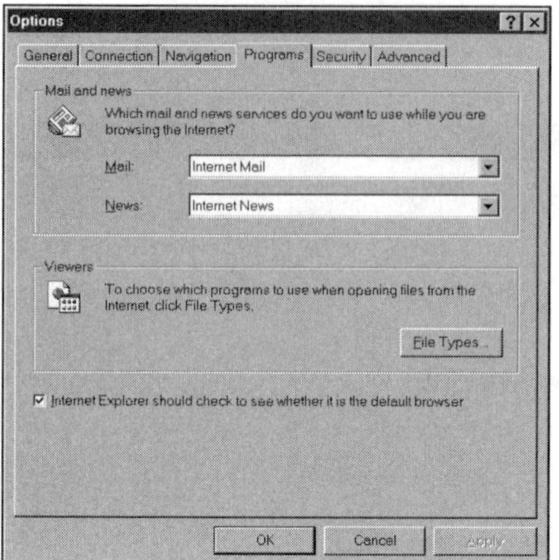

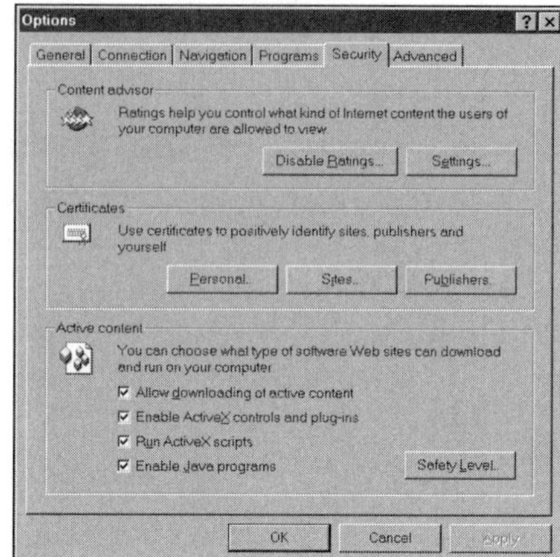

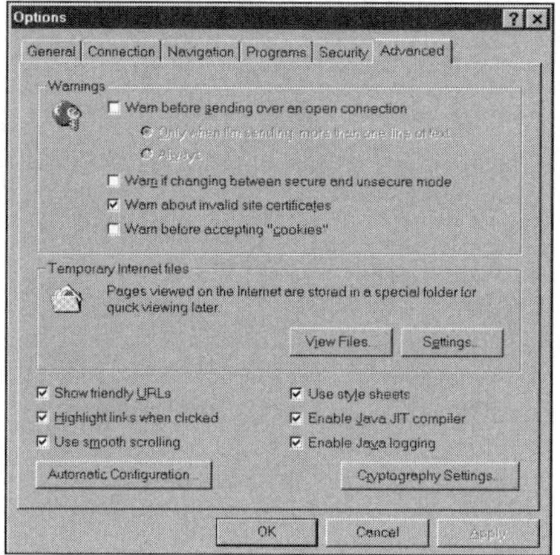

Microsoft Internet Explorer To customize the Microsoft Internet Explorer, select **Options** from the **View** menu. The option categories are listed on the "tabs" near the top of the screen: General, Connection, Navigation, Programs, Security, and Advanced.

General

The General options control the overall look of the browser.

Multimedia Some Web pages include graphics, sound, and video: the **Multimedia** section controls which special effects Internet Explorer will download from the page. If you are connected to the Internet using a modem and telephone line, you can speed up the display of Web pages

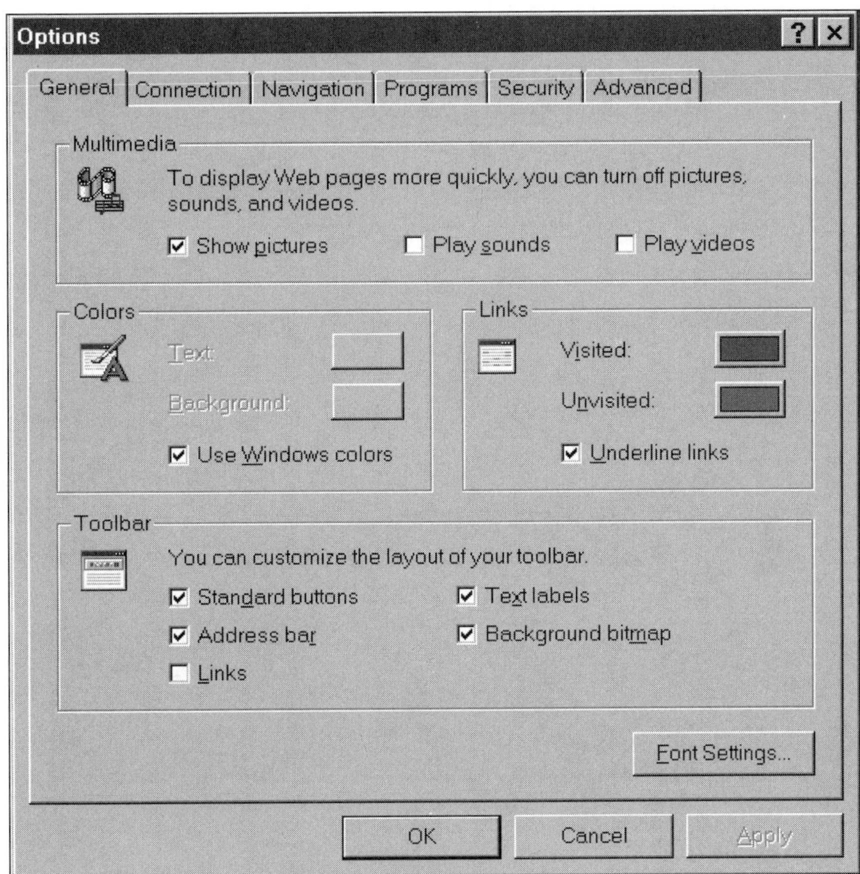

by turning *off* all three options. This is useful when you're surfing the Web and want to quickly scan pages. You won't have to wait for the multimedia effects to download to your computer; you will be able to move through pages much faster. When you find the page you're looking for, turn on the options you want.

Color, Links The **Colors** and **Links** controls allow you to customize the appearance of Web pages. These should normally be left at their default values.

Toolbar The **Toolbar** control lets you change the appearance and size of the toolbar. This is useful when you become an expert user and want to reduce the amount of screen space used by the toolbar.

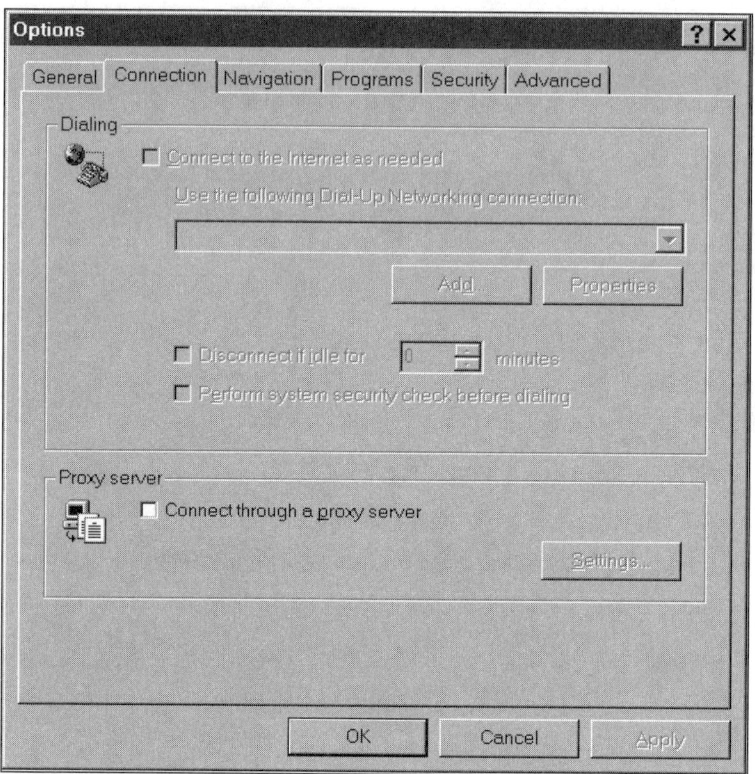

Connection

Do not change the options on the **Connection** page unless you have specific instructions to do so. These options are set by the installer of the browser. If you make any changes here incorrectly, the browser will not work.

Navigation

The Navigation page allows you to change the Start page, Search page, and links Toolbar page. You can also set the number of pages to record in the history file.

Customize The **Navigation** page lets you change the browser's "Start Page," the page that automatically displays each time the browser starts. This is useful if you always want to begin with a search engine or the Web page from a specific organization. You can also change this entry to the file "C:\WINDOWS\SYSTEM\BLANK.HTM" which is an

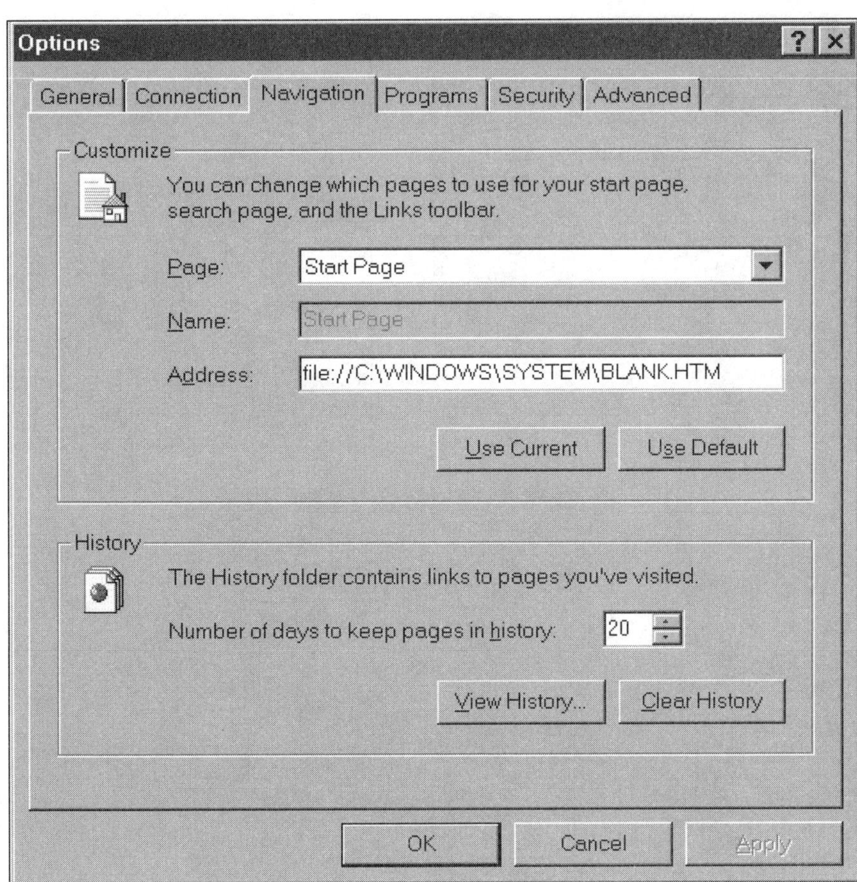

empty page. This setting makes the browser start faster and is useful when you do not stay on the same page each time you start the browser.

History The **History** section controls the amount of space the browser will use to maintain your Web page viewing history. These options are normally left at their default values unless you are given specific instructions to change them.

Programs, Advanced, and Security Pages

Do not make changes to the settings on these pages unless you are given specific instructions.

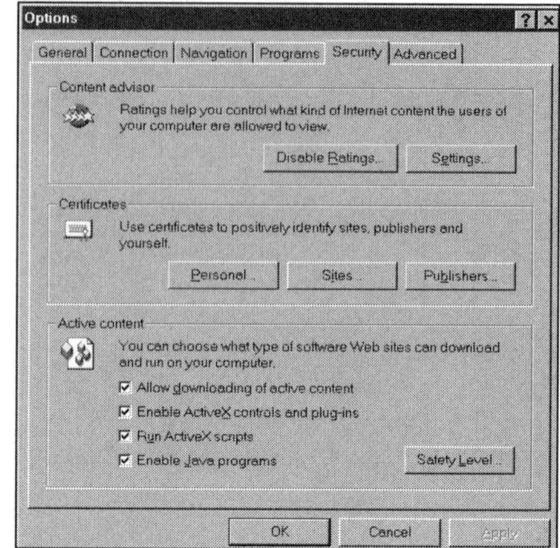

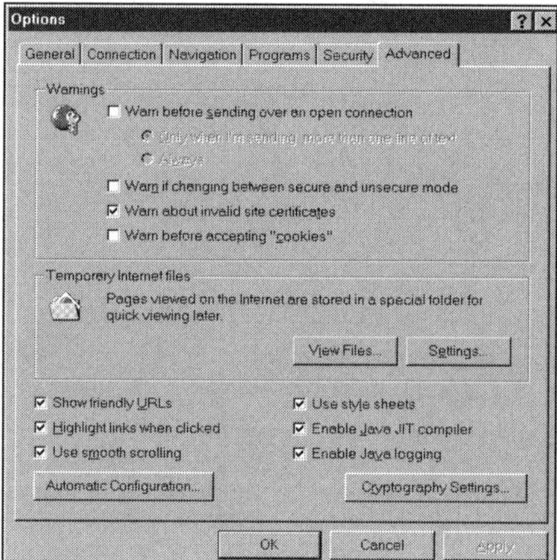

Searching for Information

When you start on a research project it's sometimes hard to know where to look for information. With so many diverse sites on the Web it would be impossible to visit them yourself looking for information. A whole new breed of programs called *search engines* will do the looking for you. A search engine looks through a giant index of Web pages which is created by robot programs that roam the Web collecting and indexing information. The index on the largest of the search sites, AltaVista (http://altavista.digital.com), contains information from 31 million pages on 476,000 Web sites. The search engine will look through this massive index for key words and phrases in a fraction of a second! AltaVista displays a link for any page that contains the words you specify anywhere on the page.

Another popular search engine is maintained by *Yahoo!* (http://www.yahoo.com), a company that maintains an index of Web sites. The *Yahoo!* search engine is based on categories and shows links to Web sites that cover topics you specify.

For health related search engines go to:

- http://www.webdirectory.com/Health/http://www.HealthAtoZ.com/
- http://www.linkmonster.com/health.html
- http://www.medexplorer.com/
- http://www.slackinc.com/matrix/
- http://www.slackinc.com/matrix/
- http://vh.radiology.uiowa.edu/Misc/Search.html

Using a Search Engine AltaVista indexes the contents of Web sites, *Yahoo!* organizes Web sites into categories. The difference in approach gives vastly different search results. *Yahoo!* returned a list of 133 categories and 12,284 sites that had the word "photo" somewhere in their title or category name. AltaVista, on the other hand, found more than 2,000,000 pages of information that use the phrase "Near-Death Experience" (there are probably a lot more, but it stops looking when it finds that many pages).

You should choose an index like *Yahoo!* when you are looking for sites that cover a specific category of information, like "Stress Management Techniques using guided imagery." Use AltaVista when there is something very specific you are looking for, like "manufacturing wrapping paper."

Simple Searches It pays to spend some time experimenting with searches and learning advanced search techniques. It's just as bad finding too much information as too little. Here's an experiment you can try with AltaVista:

1. Start Browser at AltaVista

2. Type in the word stress in the text box and click the submit button. AltaVista will search its index for all Web pages that have the word Stress. The results of your search will be returned to you in a few seconds.

part

1

3. You'll see that "Stress" was found more than 500,000 times, and "management" was found more than 6 million times. Clearly this search is not usable.

4. Now type "Stress+Management+Techniques" (with or without the quotation marks) as the search string and click **Submit.** The '+' sign is very important. It ties the words together so now AltaVista will only find sites that contain the phrase "Stress Management Techniques." This time about 400 sites are returned. That still may be too many to be of much value.

5. Now type "stress+management+techniques and guided+imagery" and click **Submit.** Because you have entered more words, the search may have more returned more sites, but this time AltaVista will organize them so the sites that have the most matching words appear first on the list. Chances are that if you were doing research on managing stress using guided imagery, you would find what you are looking for within the first few pages of links.

The moral here is to be as specific as possible when using a massive index search engine and try to trim down the number of sites returned. You will also notice that the search engines try to sort the sites they find based on the relevance of the words you specify. Each search engine uses a complicated, proprietary formula to try to bring the sites that are most likely to be of interest to the top of the list. As you scroll down the list the links will be father and farther off-topic, and there's no need to continue looking. You're better off submitting another search with a slightly different set of words and phrases to see if you can find anything else.

Now use the URL "http//www.yahoo.com" to point your browser at *Yahoo!*.

1. Type "Stress Management" in the search box and click the Search option. *Yahoo!*'s classification scheme finds 3 categories that have these words, and only 84 sites with "Stress Management" in the title.

2. Type "Stress management technique guided imagery" and click **Search.** *Yahoo!* finds fewer than 5 sites with these words in the title.

See what a difference the indexing technique makes? *Yahoo!* finds only a couple of sites that have relevant information because it's only looking at Web page titles. If a health psychologist has written an article on managing stress using guided imagery and does not include the subject in the title, *Yahoo!* won't find the page, but AltaVista will.

Try searches in both sites and see which you like best. You can also try these other search engines, one of which may be more to your liking:

Excite	http://www.excite.com
Info Seek	http://www.infoseek.com
Lycos	http://www.lycos.com
Web Crawler	http://www.webcrawler.com

Avoiding Information Overload: Advanced Search Techniques

Some of the search engines offer an *advanced* or *custom* search mode which enables you to use special commands to narrow or widen a search. The most common special commands are:

AND

Use AND to narrow a search. This command causes the search engine to find Web pages that include all of the keywords you specify. For example, the search

aerobic AND exercise

will find Web pages that use both names. A page that uses only one of these names will not be found by the search. The AND command is a great tool when you know exactly what you're looking for.

NEAR

The NEAR command is used to find any Web pages on which two words are "close" to each other. For example:

pregnant women NEAR tobacco

will find Web pages that include phrases such as "pregnant women," and "tobacco." Different search engines have different tolerances for "closeness," but the words you specify must usually be between six or eight words of each other to be found by a NEAR search.

OR

OR is used to widen a search when you're not sure how to find what you want. This command will locate all Web pages that include any of the keywords you specify. For example,

HIV OR Sexually Transmitted Diseases

part

1

will find any Web page that mentions either or both of these names. The OR command greatly increases the number of links returned by a search, so it's most often useful when you are starting a research project and want get an idea of what's available.

NOT

Careful use of NOT can narrow a search when you already know that certain keywords should be eliminated. A search like

Stress NOT post-traumatic

will find any Web page with the word "Stress" on it as long as the word "post-traumatic" is not on the same page.

These commands can also be combined. If you are going use the Web for research, it's a good investment of time to learn about these advanced search commands. Click the *Help* link in the search engine you like best to read about the various advanced searching features it offers.

Security on the Web

Avoiding Scam Artists and Credit Card Fraud Mail order catalog shopping has taken on new heights with on-line shopping via the Web. There are many on-line "storefronts" offering all types of merchandise and services for sale. Most of these operations are legitimate, but there are a few fly-by-night operators setting up Web sites. Use the same cautions you would use when shopping by mail or telephone.

- Know who you're dealing with. Be careful when dealing with companies or people you have never heard of.
- If a deal sounds too good to be true, it probably is.
- Be sure the company offers a money-back guarantee so you can return merchandise that you don't like.

There's a lot of publicity about credit card fraud on the Web, but it's not really much different than giving your credit card to a waiter in a restaurant. Someone at a store can write down your card number just as easily as the number can be recorded over the Web. The main rule is to know who you are dealing with and use some common sense. Be sure to check your credit card statements carefully if you start purchasing items over the Web.

Site Ratings Recent publicity and possible congressional action regarding the availability of pornographic and other explicit materials on the Web have resulted in a Web site rating system developed by the Recreational Software Advisory Council and enforced by the Microsoft Internet Explorer, version 3 and higher. This system, however, is totally voluntary on the part of the Web site operators, so it's by no means a foolproof system. If you want to restrict access to Web sites you find unacceptable or offensive, you should investigate the site rating system features of Internet Explorer by selecting **Options** from the **View** menu and then choosing the **Security** tag.

Virus Protection The Web offers many opportunities for you to download programs and files to your computer. Most of these programs are perfectly safe to download, but be careful when downloading programs from unknown sources. You may be ex posing your computer to a harmful virus. Be especially careful if you download games or recreational programs. If you do a lot of downloading it's worth investing in virus protection software for your computer. A virus scanner looks at programs that you have downloaded and warns you if they contain viruses before the virus has a chance to infect and damage your computer's files.

part

1

Sharing Files with Others: FTP

FTP stands for File Transfer Protocol and is the means by which you copy files from someone's computer to yours over the Internet. There are many ways of transferring files, but the easiest one is to use your Web browser.

Both Netscape Navigator and Microsoft Internet Explorer utilize FTP in two ways. The first is by downloading a file when you click a link on a Web page. Links can be set up not only to take you from one page to another, but also to start a file transfer. The second way is to use the browser to browse to an FTP site instead of a Web site.

Retrieving Files from Web Pages

When you are looking at a Web page it's not possible to distinguish browsing links from file links, except by context. Click on an FTP link to activate it. The browser will display a message box asking if you would like to save the file on your computer's disk drive, or open the file.

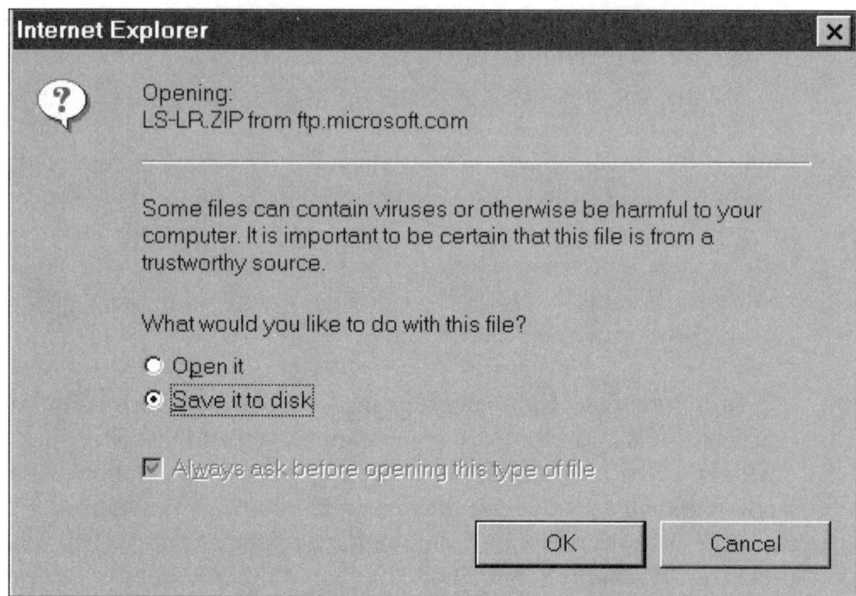

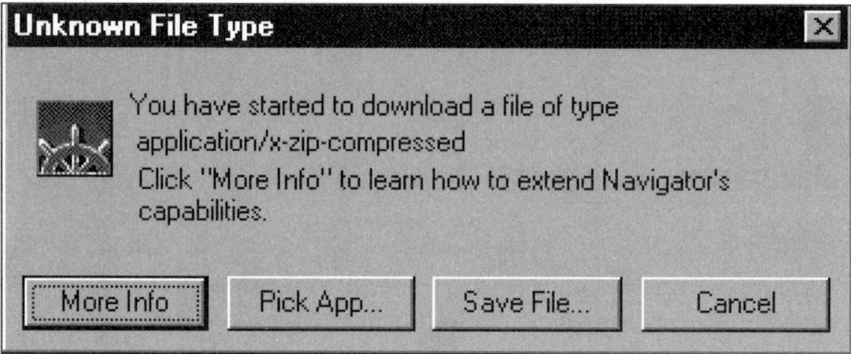

You normally choose to save the file. (If you choose to open the file instead, it will not be saved on your computer.) Choose the *Save* option and confirm the file name. After you confirm the file name a status indicator will appear on the screen.

Retrieving Files from FTP Sites

The URL for a Web site always starts with the letters "http://". For an FTP site the URL always starts with "ftp://". We're going to use Allyn & Bacon's FTP site as an example. The FTP address for Allyn & Bacon is "ftp://ftp.abacon.com". Type this address in your browser's **Go To:** or

Address: window and press the Enter key. The contents of the FTP site will appear in the browser window.

Netscape Navigator Netscape Navigator shows the structure of the FTP site by indicating files with an icon that looks like a sheet of paper with a bent corner and directories with an icon that looks like a folder. To download a file or see what's in a directory, click the highlighted link beside the icon. You will be asked if you want to save or open the file. Choose the *Save* option and the file will be sent to your computer.

Microsoft Internet Explorer Microsoft Internet Explorer shows the structure of the FTP site by putting the size next to files and the word "DIRECTORY" next to directories. To download a file or see what's in a directory click the highlighted link. Choose the *Save* option when prompted, then confirm the file name and start the download.

The status indicator will show the progress of the download. If you are connecting to the Internet using a phone line and modem, a download may take a long time—possibly hours, especially if the file is more than a few hundred thousand bytes long. Be sure you don't need the phone for while!

Posting Files You can make files available to other people by placing them on an FTP site. Each site has its own procedure for making files available, so you'll have to ask your Internet Service Provider how you can "upload" files to an FTP site so they will be available for other people.

part

1

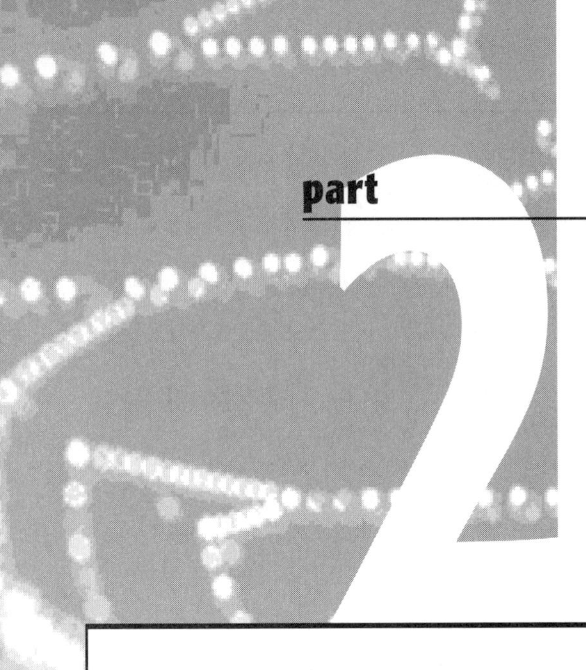

Address Book to Health Websites

The rest of this book is filled with Web sites related to all aspects of health. Each site is listed first with the URL (Universal Resource Locator) which is the Internet address. These addresses must be typed in your browser's URL text box exactly as they are shown. If any part of the URL is missing, you will not arrive where you want to go. The second part of the listings below is the title for each Web site. This is followed by a short description of what is to be found at the particular Web site.

Every listing in this book can also be accessed from the following health promotion Web page:

http://www.siu.edu/departments/bushea/

You can save yourself some time by creating a "bookmark" to this page using your Web browser.

The Web sites that follow are categorized first by the following topics: Health News, Health-Related Internet Searches, and Health-Related Journals, Magazines & Periodicals. These are followed by the following health content areas: alternative medicine and holistic health; cancer; community health; diseases; environmental health; exercise and fitness; general health; governmental and non-governmental health resources and databases; health and disease care; health education; health promotion; health psychology; heart health; injury prevention; nutrition and weight control; public health; safety; self-help and self-care; stress management; tobacco, alcohol and drug use; violence; wellness and optimum health; and women's health.

Health News

Achoo On-Line Healthcare Services—Healthcare Headline News

```
http://www.achoo.com/newspage/index.htm
```

Current news stories covering many aspects of health and healthcare. Excellent!

American Dietetic Association Press Releases

```
http://www.eatright.org/pressindex.html
```

Up to date news stories related to nutrition recently released by the ADA.

Chronic Illness OnLine News

```
http://www.chronicillnet.org/online/
```

News stories relating to chronic illnesses and disease.

CNN Food and Health News

```
http://www.cnn.com/HEALTH/index.html
```

Recent news regarding nutrition and health from science.

International Health News

```
http://www.com/healthnews/
```

This international news service has a small yearly subscription but contains excellent, up-to date information.

Mayo Clinic News

```
http://healthnet.ivi.com/ivi/mayo/common/htm/
newsstnd.htm
```

The most current information that emerges from the Mayo Clinic.

part

2

NewsPage Health and Healthcare news stories

```
http://www.newspage.com/NEWSPAGE/cgi-bin/walk.cgi/
NEWSPAGE/info/d15/
```

A topically guided page filled with health articles that are more medical and disease care oriented.

Reuters Health Information Services

```
http://www.reutershealth.com/
```

Daily News Stories on health and disease. This is an excellent "first stop" for daily health news divided into news topics for the health professional and health consumer.

The News-Times Health News

```
http://www.newstimes.com/news/today/health.htm
```

This is another daily news stories page that lists headline health stories.

USA Today Healthline

```
http://167.8.29.13/life/health/lhd1.htm
```

Health news stories from USA today.

Wellness Newsletter Weekly

```
http://www.wellmedia.com/news.html
```

Stories and articles mostly on items that are wellness related.

Yahoo! Health News Daily

```
http://www.yahoo.com/headlines/health/
```

Yahoo!'s news section on daily health stories. Another excellent "first stop" for daily health news.

Your Health Daily

```
http://nytsyn.com/med/
```

Daily health-related news stories from the New York Times.

Health-Related Searches

AltaVista Health Topics Search

```
http://www.altavista.digital.com/
```

Type the word(s)you want to search in the box when you arrive at this excellent search engine.

Environmental Organization Web Directory Search–"Health"

```
http://www.webdirectory.com/Health/
```

This is a good search engine that browses the Web for sites that are a bit more related to environmental health.

Excite Search–"Health and Medicine"

```
http://www.excite.com/Reviews/Health_and_Medicine/
?a-Rf-t
```

Click on one of the health sub-topics or use the text box to type in the word(s) for which you would like to search.

Galaxy Search–"Health"

```
http://www.einet.net/galaxy/Community/Health.html
```

On arriving at this search engine, click on one of the health subtopics or search through the other health resources such as health articles, events, periodicals, discussion groups, directories, and organizations.

Health A to Z

```
http://www.HealthAtoZ.com/
```

This is an excellent health search—by category or by wordsearch. It includes a large list of health topics which link to many related Web sites.

Infoseek Guide Search–"Health"

```
http://guide-p.infoseek.com//DB?tid=1207&db=0&sv=
IS&lk=noframes
```

This link is designed to be a Web search for all results under the general topic "health." You may make adjustments for additional searching once you have looked at this output. You may also choose from one of the health subtopics listed on the side.

LinkMonster Health Catalogue

```
http://www.linkmonster.com/health.html
```

Another great health search. Contains some sites that are related to businesses that deal with health products.

Lycos Search—"Health and Medicine"

```
http://a2z.lycos.com/Health_and_Medicine/
```

Click on one of the health sub-topics or type in the word(s) for which you would like to search.

Magellan Search—"Health and Medicine"

```
http://www.mckinley.com/magellan/Reviews/
Health_and_Medicine/index.magellan.html
```

Click on one of the health sub-topics or type in the word(s) for which you would like to search.

MedExplorer

```
http://www.medexplorer.com/
```

Dedicated to providing a Web site search engine solely for medical/health-related Web sites. Only medical/health-related sites will be returned to you.

Medical Matrix

```
http://www.kumc.edu:80/mmatrix/
```

This search engine is a guide to Internet Clinical Medicine Resources. It is a HUGE Resource for medicine and disease care.

Point Search—"health and medicine"

```
http://www.pointcom.com/categories/health/
```

This page has several health categories that have searched the Internet for Web sites that have been rated by content, presentation, or just listed alphabetically. The results of these searches will bring you the best "out there" on health.

MetaSearch

```
http://www.stpt.com/
```

This is a meta-search engine that will place the word you type in this box into all of the major search engines.

Virtual Hospital

```
http://vh.radiology.uiowa.edu/Misc/Search.html
```

With this search engine, simply type the keyword(s)in the box. This engine is designed to be more medically oriented.

WebCrawler Health Topics Search

```
http://www.webcrawler.com/select/med.new.html
```

Choose from one of the displayed topics or click "search" and type in the health topic that you seek.

Yahoo! Search–"Health"

```
http://www.yahoo.com/Health/
```

This site allows you to use the popular *Yahoo!* search engine to seek health information. Choose one of the health categories listed or type a subject in the box and then push the "search" button next to the text box.

Health-Related Journals, Magazines and Periodicals

All About Health

```
http://www.allabouthealth.com/
```

All About Health features the latest research findings from universities and research centers worldwide, events, the latest and greatest books and software, new and exciting health-related products, articles, regular columns, thousands of links, plus lots more.

Aesclepian Chronicles

```
http://www.forthrt.com/~chronicl/homepage.html
```

The goal of the Aesclepian Chronicles is to publish informative and in-spirational articles about the many new complementary and allopathic treatment modalities that are emerging. These modalities may be ap-proached from both a personal and a clinical perspective from the Insti-tute of Synergistic Medicine.

Alive Wellness Newsletter

```
http://carlisle-www.army.mil/apfri/alive.htm
```

The ALIVE wellness newsletter is a product of the Army Physical Fitness Research Institute, U.S. Army War College, Carlisle Barracks, PA.

Balance: Fitness on the Net

```
http://ww2.hyperlink.com/balance/
```

This is an excellent monthly electronic magazine covering all aspects of fitness, exercise, lifestyle, nutrition and sports.

Body Mind Spirit On-line Magazine

```
http://www.hinman.oro.net/~bmsweb/bmsmag.htm
```

Body Mind Spirit magazine seeks to contribute to the evolution of a new consciousness, in which spiritual seeking and natural living provide the path to a more fulfilling, meaningful life.

Fitness Partner

```
http://www.cdc.net/~primus/fpc/fpcjs70.htm#10
```

This page is a long and very fine collection of magazines, journals, arti-cles, and newsletters on-line. They relate primarily to fitness but also look at many other aspects of health.

Lifelines Newsletter

```
http://www.lifelines.com/lifenews.html
```

A publication that encourages better health and a better life.

Mayo Clinic Newsletter On-Line

```
http://healthnet.ivi.com/ivi/mayo/common/htm/
library.htm
```

Monthly articles and news items. Very timely articles from the Mayo clinic.

The Medical Reporter

```
http://www.dash.com/netro/nwx/tmr/tmr.html
```

A monthly educational health magazine on the World Wide Web for enlightened healthcare consumers. Published solely in cyberspace since April of 1995, The Medical Reporter emphasizes preventive medicine, primary care, patient advocacy, education and support, as well as topics in sub-specialty medicine of interest to men and women.

part
2

Medscape

```
http://www.medscape.com/
```

For health professionals and interested consumers, this newsletter features thousands of full-text, peer-reviewed articles, medical news, Medline, and interactive quizzes. Updated daily, and free!

Men's Fitness On-Line

```
http://mensfitness.com/
```

On-line rendition of the magazine bearing the same name.

New Frontier: Magazine of Transformation

```
http://www.newfrontier.com/
```

Monthly editions of an on-line newsletter dedicated to promoting high levels of health and wellness.

New Age Journal On-Line

```
http://www.newage.com/
```

New Age Journal is committed to uncovering traditional wisdom and integrating it with modern technology. New Age Journal provides more than merely simple information. It is a magazine of insight and perspective, covering people and issues often ignored by the mainstream, and uncovering trends not yet discovered by the more popular press.

New England Journal of Medicine On-Line

```
http://www.nejm.org/
```

This is a weekly journal reporting the results of important medical research worldwide.

Nutrition Action Healthletter

```
http://www.cspinet.org/nah/
```

A Health letter published by the Center for Science in the Public Interest.

One Excellent List of Health Journals and Periodicals

```
http://pie.org/E21221T3783
```

Here is another list of on-line health and medical journals.

The Share Guide Holistic Health Journal and Directory

```
http://www.shareguide.com/mag/
```

This page is a magazine focusing on holistic health, personal growth and environmental awareness. Their goal is to make information available for people actively working to improve themselves and the planet.

The Townsend Letter For Doctors and Patients

```
http://www.thorne.com/townsend.html
```

This is another newsletter on health that is a bit more medically oriented.

Wellness Wise Electronic Journal

```
http://nansen.jhuapl.edu/wej/
```

A health journal covering preventive and lifestyle medicine.

Yoga Journal

```
http://www.yogajournal.com
```

This is a is a journal dedicated to communicating, to as broad an audience as possible, the qualities of being that yoga exemplifies: peace, integrity, clarity, and compassion.

Alternative Medicine and Holistic Health

A topical index of alternative health care

```
http://sunsite.sut.ac.jp/arch/academic/medicine/alter
native-healthcare/
```

Links to information on many aspects of alternative medicine including massage, meditation, herbal therapy, and ayurvedic medicine.

Acupuncture.com

```
http://www.Acupuncture.com/
```

Traditional oriental therapies along with related resources for consumers, practitioners, and students. Includes other related information and links as well.

Alternative Medicine Homepage

```
http://www.pitt.edu/~cbw/altm.html
```

A jumpstation for sources of information on unconventional, unorthodox, unproven, or alternative, complementary, innovative, integrative therapies.

Buffalo Springboard

```
http://www.quake.net/~xdcrlab/hp.html
```

Links to sources of information, advice and articles for alternative health.

Herb Research (Foundation) News

```
http://sunsite.unc.edu/herbs/
```

Research and education on worldwide use of herbs for health, environmental conservation, and international development.

Holistic Healing Web Page

```
http://www.tiac.net/users/mgold/health.html
```

Extensive holistic health-related information including articles, Web links, group links and mailing information lists.

Interlude Links

```
http://www.nursery.com/~interlud/links.htm
```

Websites that are good for you!

The International Society for the Enhancement of Eyesight

```
http://ezinfo.ucs.indiana.edu/~aeulenbe/i_see
```

A Web site and contents of a mailing list dedicated to promoting better natural eyesight for everyone!

Medweb: Alternative Medicine

```
http://www.gen.emory.edu/MEDWEB/keyword/
alternative_medicine.html
```

Extensive resourse for links to information and sites for alternative medicine.

Natural Medicine, Complementary Health Care and Alternative Therapies

```
http://www.teleport.com/~amrta/
```

Links and resources for education in organizations, news, and programs for alternative medicine.

Oxygen and Ozone Therapies

```
http://www.oxytherapy.com/
```

Information on oxygen therapies including, the use of hydrogen perox-
ide, ozone therapy, hyperbaric oxygen, stabilized oxygen, and ionization.

Spirituality and Consciousness

```
http://zeta.cs.adfa.oz.au/Spirituality.html
```

Resource page with instruction, links and sites for spiritual health and
well-being.

Spirit WWW

```
More http://www.spiritweb.org/
```

Spirituality Resources on the WWW including links to manifold forms
of spirituality.

Wellness Links

```
http://wellmedia.com/links.html
```

Links to many Web sites relating to holistic thinking, spirituality, and
personal development.

Cancer

American Cancer Society

```
http://www.cancer.org/
```

Official homepage for the ACS concerning the symptoms, treatment, and
prevention of cancer.

Breast Cancer Information Clearinghouse

```
http://nysernet.org/bcic/
```

A Web site designed to provide information for breast cancer patients
and their families.

Cancer News on the Net

`http://www.cancernews.com/`

This site is dedicated to bringing patients and their families the latest information on cancer diagnosis and treatment.

CanSearch

`http://www.access.digex.net/~mkragen/cansearch.html`

The purpose of this guide is to assist those not experienced in finding sources on the Net to go to cancer resources quickly and find answers to their questions or at least become more informed patients and caretakers.

JOMOL Cancer Research Information

`http://africa.com/~martin/jomol/`

Information on an alternative therapy for cancer.

National Cancer Institute

`http://www.nci.nih.gov/`

Complete information source of the National Cancer Institute. The National Cancer Institute (NCI) is a component of the National Institutes of Health (NIH), one of eight agencies that compose the Public Health Service (PHS) in the Department of Health and Human Services (DHHS). The NCI, established under the National Cancer Act of 1937, is the Federal Government's principal agency for cancer research and training.

National Comprehensive Cancer Network

`http://www.cancer.med.umich.edu/NCCN/NCCN.html`

The NCCN was formed to create cancer-management strategies for large employers and third-party payers. Its mission is to integrate the experience of member cancer centers to ensure delivery of high-quality, cost-effective services to cancer patients across the country.

Skin Cancer Information Page

`http://www.maui.net/~southsky/introto.html`

A very thorough information page on skin cancer. Designed to be a gathering place for all available information about skin cancer and related subjects.

Steve Dunn's Cancer Information page

```
http://cancerguide.org/
```

A very informative guide dedicated to helping you find the answers to your questions about cancer, and especially to helping you find the questions you need to ask.

University of Pennsylvania Cancer Resource

```
http://www.oncolink.upenn.edu/
```

An extensive Web site touted as the first multimedia oncology information resource placed on the Internet.

Community Health

American Heart Association National Center

```
http://www.amhrt.org/
```

The American Heart Association is one of the world's premier health organizations, and is committed to reducing disability and death from cardiovascular diseases and stroke. This site provides a wealth of information about almost 300 subjects from the American Heart Association.

Center for Disease Control and Prevention

```
http://www.cdc.gov/cdc.html
```

The CDC's mission is to promote health and quality of life by preventing and controlling disease, injury, and disability. This site contains links to other agencies, and a lot of information on various health-related topics such as, the CDC, health information, travelers' health, publications and products, data and statistics, training and employment, and funding.

Coummunity Health Concepts Home Page

```
http://web.indstate.edu/hlthsfty/hlth221/chhome.htm
```

This page includes a college course outline with excellent information and a huge list of community health-related links that accompany this excellent course.

Escoffery's Health Education Page

```
http://userwww.service.emory.edu/~cescoff/cam.html
```

A jumpsite to resources on Certified Health Education Specialist (C. H. E. S.), professional organizations, health education/public health conference calendar, health information resources, health education and promotion listservs, public health software, schools of public health, health resources, and state health addresses on the Internet.

National Clearinghouse for Alcohol and Drug Information

```
http://www.health.org/
```

NCADI is the information service of the Center for Substance Abuse Prevention of the U.S. Department of Health & Human Services. NCADI is the world's largest resource for current information and materials concerning substance abuse prevention.

NewsFile

```
http://www.homepage.holowww.com/
```

This site contains references and abstracts to journal articles that relate to public and community health. Excellent resource for research.

Pan American Health Organization

```
http://www.paho.org/
```

PAHO's mission is to cooperate technically with the member countries and to stimulate cooperation among them in order that, while maintaining a healthy environment and charting a course to sustainable human development, the peoples of the Americas may achieve health for all and by all.

World Health Organization

```
http://www.who.ch/
```

The objective of WHO is the attainment by all peoples of the highest possible level of health. Health, as defined in the WHO Constitution, is a state of complete physical, mental and social well-being and not merely the absence of disease or infirmity.

Diseases: Chronic and Acute

A2Z Search—Illness and Disorders

```
http://a2z.lycos.com/Health_and_Medicine/Illnesses_an
d_Disorders/
```

A Web search for information by disease categories using the engine called A2Z.

American Diabetes Association

```
http://www.diabetes.org/
```

This is the homepage of the American Diabetes Association. Their mission is to prevent and cure diabetes and to improve the lives of all people affected by diabetes.

American Lung Association

```
http://www.lungusa.org/noframes/
```

This is the ALA on-line resource for information on asthma and other lung diseases, tobacco control, and environmental health.

CDC Diseases Page

```
http://www.cdc.gov/diseases/diseases.html
```

Information on many diseases in the United States including data on incidence and prevalence of diseases.

part

2

Chronic Illness-Net

http://www.chronicillnet.org/

This Web site describes itself as the first multimedia information source on the Internet dedicated to chronic illnesses including AIDS, cancer, Persian Gulf War Syndrome, autoimmune diseases, Chronic Fatigue Syndrome, heart disease and neurological diseases.

Diseases, Disorders, and Related Topics

http://www.mic.ki.se/Diseases/index.html

Resources on the Internet for laypersons, health care professionals and scientists. Gigantic Resource—excellent place to begin searching for disease related information.

Dyke's Library: Selected Chronic Disease Information for Patients

http://www.kumc.edu/service/dykes/RRPAGES/patient/pchronic.html

This site provides easy access to the full text of AHCPR supported clinical practice guidelines that have been written for consumers.

Med Help General Library

http://medhlp.netusa.net/

This page links to thousands (seemingly) of articles covering a wide variety of diseases, conditions, and health concerns.

National Center for Chronic Disease Prevention and Health Promotion

http://ftp.cdc.gov/nccdphp/nccdhome.htm

A page devoted to consolidating National Centers for Disease Control and Prevention (CDC) efforts in chronic disease prevention and health promotion.

On-Line Allergy Center

http://www.sig.net/~allergy/welcome.html

Browse through these pages for helpful information on the relief of a variety of symptoms including: . . . nasal congestion . . . eye redness/ soreness . . . sneezing . . . wheezing . . . coughing . . . joint pain . . . intestinal pain . . . skin rashes/irritation . . . itching . . . yeast infections . . . mood swings . . . hyperactivity . . . attention deficit disorder . . . fatigue.

Point Search's top 5%

```
http://point.lycos.com/reviews/database/hmil_e.html
```

Point Communication lists and describes the top Web sites around the world that are disease related.

Virology WWW server

```
http://www.bocklabs.wisc.edu/Welcome.html
```

This Web site is a huge resource collecting all possible information related to viruses including maps of viruses, digitized images of viruses, conferences, news and journals, links, emerging Infectious Diseases and more.

Environmental Health

Agency for Toxic Substances and Disease Registry

```
http://atsdr1.atsdr.cdc.gov:8080/cx.html
```

A simple guide to search the World Wide Web for environmental health information. The primary focus is to find and share global information resources with the public on the linkage between human exposure to hazardous chemicals and adverse human health effects.

Environmental Health Resource Page

```
http://clas.www.pdx.edu/~willert/EnvHealth.html
```

Quick and easy access for the public to general information about environmental health including environmental homepages, newsgroups, journals, and databases.

National Center for Environmental Health (NCEH)

```
http://www.cdc.gov/nceh/0ncehhom.htm
```

The mission of the NCEH is to provide national leadership, through science and service, to promote health and quality of life by preventing and controlling disease, birth defects, disability, and death resulting from interactions between people and their environment.

National Institute of Environmental Health Sciences

```
http://www.niehs.nih.gov/
```

NIEHS mission is to reduce the burden of human illness and dysfunction from environmental causes by understanding each of these elements and how they interrelate. The NIEHS achieves its mission through multidisciplinary biomedical research programs, prevention and intervention efforts, and communication strategies that encompass training, education, technology transfer, and community outreach.

Project NatureConnect

```
http://www.pacificrim.net/~nature/
```

This page is especially for nature enthusiasts. The designers of this page created this site to help others promote a profoundly heightened sense of self worth and environmental responsibility.

Exercise and Fitness

American Alliance for Health, Physical Education, Recreation, and Dance

```
http://www.aahperd.org/
```

AAHPERD's homepage includes links to American Association for Active Lifestyles and Fitness, American Association for Health Education, American Association for Leisure and Recreation, National Association for Girls and Women in Sport, National Association for Sport and Physical Education, and the National Dance Association.

American College of Sports Medicine

```
http://www.a1.com/sportsmed/
```

This is the homepage of the largest, most respected sports medicine and exercise science organization in the world.

British Columbia Physical Education Specialists Association (PEPSA)

```
http://www.etc.bc.ca/~dsamulak/
```

PEPSA provides leadership, advocacy and resources for physical education teachers in order to assist in the implementaton of Quality Daily Physical Education.

Fitness and Exercise Frequently Asked Questions

```
ftp://ftp.cray.com/pub/misc.fitness/misc.fitness.
faq.html
```

Information and answers to questions concerning fitness, weight loss, weight training, and exercise.

Fitness for a Healthy Heart

```
http://hyrax.med.uth.tmc.edu/ptnt/00000384.htm
```

Simple ways to include fitness into normal daily activities and routines.

Fitness Products Council

```
http://www.sportlink.com/fitness/
```

Contains a Speakers Bureau, market research reports, a newsletter, and the Surgeon General's recent report on health, fitness, and exercise.

FitnessWorld Home Page

```
http://www.fitnessworld.com/
```

A wealth of excellent information on fitness.

part
2

Exercise and Fitness

```
http://www.welltech.com/net_connect/fit.html
```

Several high quality links to exercise and fitness information.

Exercise, Fitness and Pregnancy

```
http://www.noah.cuny.edu/pregnancy/march_of_dimes/pre
_preg.plan/fit42is.html
```

A lot of information on excersise and pregnancy, including benefits, risks and guidelines.

Exercise, Fitness and Big Folks

```
http://www.comlab.ox.ac.uk/oucl/users/sharon.curtis/B
igFolks/fitres_FAQ.html
```

This document contains information about exercise and fitness equipment and clothing for fat people. The makers of this page describe it as a source of information for the fat folks who do want to exercise.

Fitness Partner

```
http://www.cdc.net/~primus/fpc/fpchome.html
```

Excellent jumpsite to fitness, health and nutrition related information on the Web.

International Society of Biomechanics

```
http://www.kin.ucalgary.ca/isb/index.html
```

Here you will find information about the ISB, biomechanical software and data contributed by members, and pointers to other sources of bio-mechanics-related information.

The Kinesiology Worldwide Home Page

```
http://www.umich.edu/~divkines/kinesworld/
```

A jumpsite to many kinesiology-related Web sites around the world.

National Coalition for Promoting Physical Activity

```
http://www.ncppa.org/
```

This is a premier organization in the country to promote physical activity. The objective of NCPPA is to unite the strengths of public, private and industry efforts into a collaborative partnership to inspire Americans to lead physically active lifestyles to enhance their health and quality of life.

The Running Page

```
http://sunsite.unc.edu/drears/running/running.html
```

The Running Page contains information about upcoming races, race results, places to run, running related products, magazines, and other information.

Stretching and Flexibility

```
http://www.cs.huji.ac.il/papers/rma/
stretching_toc.html
```

Excellent information on increasing our understanding of the benefits and methods of stretching out and increasing flexibility.

Weightlifting Page

```
http://www.cs.unc.edu/~kyle/weights.html
```

Excellent resources on sports nutrition, fitness and weightlifting, including, Olympic-style weightlifting, powerlifting, bodybuilding, etc.

WWW Women's Sports Page

```
http://fiat.gslis.utexas.edu/~lewisa/womsprt.html
```

An excellent jumpsite to women's sports pages around the WWW. Some of the topics include womens sports, womens sports organizations, and issues in womens sports.

WorldGuide Health and Fitness Forum

```
http://www.worldguide.com/Fitness/hf.html
```

Information on anatomy, strength training, cardiovascular exercise, eating well, sports medicine, etc.

General Health

Duke University Healthy Devil: on-line

```
http://h-devil-www.mc.duke.edu/h-devil
```

A general health resource location from Duke University. Contains a large list of health topics with basic definitions.

Gateway Health Enterprises

```
http://www.localweb.com/gateway/
```

Their Web page describes itself as a company dedicated to educating consumers about healthy lifestyles, empowering them to be proactive in the maintenance of health and well-being, and supporting organizations that cater to the health needs of their customers or employees.

Galaxy-Health

```
http://galaxy.einet.net/galaxy/Community/Health.html
```

This Web site is a galaxy search for community health topics and links

Go Ask Alice

```
http://www.cc.columbia.edu:80/cu/healthwise/
```

Interactive answers to questions on various health topics

Hardin Meta Directory for Internet Health Information

```
http://www.arcade.uiowa.edu/hardin-www/md.html
```

Pointers to the most complete and frequently cited lists in many health subjects—a bit more medically oriented, but good.

Healthtouch

```
http://www.healthtouch.com/
```

Information on dozens of health topics and diseases as well as a medication guide on drug uses, precautions, and side effects.

The Longevity Game

```
http://www.northwesternmutual.com/longevit/
longevit.htm
```

See how old you'll be before you pass on.

Men's health issues page

```
http://www.vix.com/men/health/health.html
```

This is a huge resource on most health aspects relating more specifically to men.

National Council Against Health Fraud, Inc. (NCAHF)

```
http://www.ncahf.org/
```

These folks are the health information watchdogs. NCAHF is a non-profit, tax-exempt voluntary health agency that focuses its attention on health fraud, misinformation and quackery as public health problems.

National Institutes of Health

```
http://www.nih.gov
```

Homepage for NIH.

National Health Information Center (NHIC)

```
http://nhic-nt.health.org/
```

The Health Information Resource Database includes 1,100 organizations and government offices that provide health information on request. Entries include contact information, short abstracts, and information about publications and services the organizations provide.

On-line Health Topics

```
http://www.ihr.com/topics.html
```

This page contains more pointers to interesting and useful health information.

part 2

The Wellness Interactive Network

```
http://www.stayhealthy.com/
```

Self described as a Web site with access to thousands of Health Information Resources on the Internet.

Yahoo! "Health" Search Results

```
http://www.yahoo.com/Health
```

Contains links to health sites of all types, shapes, and sizes.

Government and Non-Government Health Resources and Databases

CDC Wonder

```
http://wwwonder.cdc.gov/
```

This page provides a single point of access to a variety of CDC reports, guidelines, and even numeric public health data.

Government WWW Sites useful to Health Administrators

```
http://atl1.mercer.edu/www/health/health.html
```

This page is mostly geared toward health and health care administration. It includes links to most of the governmental health agencies.

HealthLaw: Government Agencies

```
http://www.ljextra.com/practice/health/hegov.html
```

Up to date news on national health issues from a legal point of view. Includes a large list of government health agencies.

(IHPP) Intergovernmental Health Policy Project

```
http://www.ncsl.org/ihpp/
```

Since 1979, the Intergovernmental Health Policy Project has been America's only independent, university-based organization devoted solely to research and reporting on health care policy at the state and local levels.

Morbidity and Mortality Weekly Report

```
http://www.cdc.gov/epo/mmwr/mmwr.html
```

The Morbidity and Mortality Weekly Report (MMWR) Series is prepared by the Centers for Disease Control and Prevention (CDC) and are based on weekly reports to CDC by state health departments.

National Center for Health Statistics

```
http://www.cdc.gov/nchswww/nchshome.htm
```

The mission of the National Center for Health Statistics (NCHS) is to provide statistical information that will guide actions and policies to improve the health of the American people. As the nation's principal health statistics agency, NCHS leads the way with accurate, relevant, and timely data.

Health and Disease Care

part

2

American Hospital Publishing, Inc.

```
http://www.AmHPI.com/
```

Publishes Hospitals & Health Networks, AHA News, Materials Management in Health Care, Health Facilities Management and other health care things.

AMSO Managed Care Forum

```
http://www.amso.com/
```

AMSO provides the provider community with management services that facilitate the health care professionals role and sophistication in the managed health care marketplace. Whether you are a health care professional, executive, or a concerned health care consumer, this Web site will help you make better informed decisions about the managed care issues confronting you.

Convergent Medical Systems

```
http://www.convergentmedical.com/
```

This site has information relating to: healthcare consultants, strategic management, managed care, health policy planning, health insurance, medical education, medical regulation, health promotion, wellness programs, allied health professions, alternative and complementary medicine, and world medicine.

GlobalMedic

```
http://www.globalmedic.com/
```

Empowering Healthcare Users Through Education and Prevention. This interesting site include a Medical Encyclopedia, nutrition information, and health information for women and children.

Health Care Liability Alliance

```
http://www.wp.com/HCLA/
```

HCLA is a national advocacy coalition that supports effective federal health care liability reform to enhance the fairness, timeliness and cost-effectiveness of the civil justice system in resolving health care injury disputes.

Health Care Resource Links

```
http://www.microserve.net/~csi/HealthLinks.HTML
```

This site contains links to various health care sites and other reference sources including demographic databases for use by not-for-profit health care organizations within the U.S.

LIFE: Life and Health Insurance Information Site

```
http://www.life-line.org/site1.cgi
```

An excellent educational site designed to provide you with straightforward, unbiased information on life and health insurance.

Medscape

```
http://www5.medscape.com/Home/About.mhtml#Mission
```

Medscape pools information from clinical journals, medical news providers, medical education programs, and material created expressly for Medscape. The result is a medical Web site rich in content, broad in appeal, and high in quality.

Opus Communication's HealthWave

```
http://www.opuscomm.com/
```

A Healthcare Resource Provider. This page contains interesting resources on many things related to health care.

State and National Healthcare Organizations

```
http://www.ihr.com/natlorg.html
```

Developed by Internet Health Resources. This page contains references to organizations involved with health and health care.

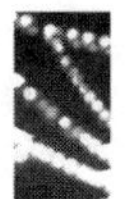

Health Education

American Cancer Society: Comprehensive School Health

```
http://www.cancer.org/cshe.html
```

Excellent resource for information on school health education.

ERIC Clearinghouse on Teaching and Teacher Education: Health, Physical Education, Recreation and Dance Divisions

```
http://www.ericsp.org/hprdtoc.html
```

This is a great site for information and Internet resources for teachers, teachers organizations, publications, financial aid, professional development schools, educational materials and resources for educators in Health, Physical Education, Recreation and Dance.

The Health Education Hitlist

```
http://www.ex.ac.uk/~dregis/healthy.html
```

A jumpsite to World Wide Web pages for those interested in health education including indices and search engines, school health resource services, health education, health care, public health, and other health issues.

Health Education Professional Resources (HEPR)

```
http://www.nyu.edu/education/health/healthed/taub/
hepr/frames/index.html
```

Extensive resource site for Health Education Professionals.

Health Promotion

Association for Worksite Health Promotion

```
http://www.awhp.com/
```

AWHP is a not-for-profit network of worksite health promotion professionals dedicated to sharing the best-of-practice methods, processes and technologies. Site includes information on AWHP as well as other resources and links to wellness, health and fitness pages.

Monash Health Promotion on the Internet

```
http://www.monash.edu.au/health/
```

Australia's Monash University's page on health promotion. It features a health promotion interactive lounge, information and sites for the following; patient education, calander of health events, Internet health directory, health resources, and health promotion research and education.

Rural Health Resources

```
http://www.siu.edu/~crhssd/rhres.htm
```

SIU center for Rural Health and Social Service Development. An excellent site with information and links to many great resources including, rural health resources, health agencies, medical resources, publications, socioeconomic data resources, search engines, Web page and HTML help guides.

WellTech International

```
http://www.welltech.com/
```

One of the best resources for information and links for health promotion and wellness professionals.

Health Psychology

American Psychological Association

`http://www.apa.org`

This is the homepage of the APA. It includes the newspaper of the American Psychological Association, as well as other links and information to books, journals, employment, and public, practice and education information and much more.

At Health Inc.

`http://www.athealth.com/`

A site designed to connect mental health professionals and those they serve with the power and the resources of the Internet.

Centre for Psychotherapeutic Studies

`http://www.shef.ac.uk/~psysc/psychotherapy/index.html`

You can search all of the major mental health resources on the World Wide Web from one page; connect to all 857 psychology, psychiatry, neuroscience and social science journals and journal search engines; locate mental health texts, search for a colleague, a quotation, an electronic book, define a word, find a synonym, consult an electronic biography or connect to all of the major Internet search engines. This site is remarkable!

Consciousness/Parapsychology/Transpersonal Psychology

`http://www.uwsp.edu/acad/psych/dk/danielpg.htm`

This is a page of psychological information specifically in the areas of consciousness, altered states of consciousness, parapsychology and transpersonal psychology.

Dr. John Grohol's Mental Health Page

`http://www.coil.com/~grohol/`

This site is in the top 5% of all Web sites. A very good psychological resource site for psychology, support, and mental health issues, resources and people.

Magic Stream

```
http://fly.hiwaay.net/~garson/
```

Journal of Emotional Wellness. The Web Dex contains extensive links on topics such as: addictions, recovery, child abuse, fitness, nutrition, depression, family, etc. The Journal contains original poetry, essays, articles and short stories focused on personal growth and the universal in human emotion.

MedWeb: Mental Health, Psychiatry, Psychology

```
http://www.gen.emory.edu/MEDWEB/keyword/mental_health
~psychiatry~psychology.html
```

Excellent and extensive sites and resources for many aspects of mental health information.

Mental Health Net

```
http://www.cmhc.com/
```

An excellent starting point for psychological information on the Internet. MHN's goal is to provide you with an easy-to-use, friendly resource in which to access all the mental health topics on the Internet.

Pie On-line

```
http://pie.org/E18634T3783
```

Top mental and health Web sites for associations, foundations, government, health publications, mental health, public policy, research institutes, Web gateways, cool sites, search the Net links, and Pie homepage.

Psychology Links

```
http://www.psyunix.iupui.edu/psych_dir.html
```

Links to organizations, journals, departments and other resources having to do with psychology.

Sleep Medicine Home Page

```
http://www.cloud9.net/~thorpy/
```

This home page lists resources regarding all aspects of sleep including, the physiology of sleep, clinical sleep medicine, sleep research, federal and state information, patient information, and business-related groups.

Heart Health

Can Heart Disease Really Be Prevented?

```
http://www.cardio.com/articles/preventn.htm
```

By Peter M. Abel M.D. Medical Director, Prevention Center for Cardiovascular Disease Cardiovascular Institute of the South/Morgan City. Excellent information and sites to many other resources on heart disease.

Cardiovascular Institute of the South

```
http://www.cardio.com/
```

CIS, a leading center for the advanced diagnosis and treatment of heart and circulatory disease, presents a wide-ranging library of doctor column-style reports on this vital and rapidly evolving aspect of medicine.These reports cover the full spectrum of prevention, diagnosis, nonsurgical and surgical treatment of circulatory problems.

Healthy Heart

```
http://sln.fi.edu/biosci/healthy/healthy.html
```

Excellent information on a wide range of subjects pertaining to a healthy heart including educational and enrichment activities.

Heart Institute

```
http://www.iea.com/~tcantre/education.html
```

Heart Education Page from Spokane's Education Department. Includes interesting facts and information on heart disease, risk factors, heart terminology, healthy eating at home and in restaurants and other projects.

Heart Surgery Forum

```
http://www.hsforum.com/heartsurgery/home.hsf
```

This Web site is a complete information center for the field of Cardiac Surgery and related disciplines. It contains cutting edge information on heart disease and heart surgery. This page is a bit more medically oriented than others but is still very interesting.

Late breaking news for heart health

```
http://www.mindspring.com/~mtm/news.html
```

This sites is dedicated to natural health, alternative medicine, and the latest available news related to the improvement of overall health of men and women over 35.

Linus C. Pauling

```
http://www.internetwks.com/pauling/
```

This is an interesting Web page on reversing heart disease without surgury (extensive info-site). It follows many of the theories and ideas espoused by the late Linus Pauling.

The Learning Center

```
http://www.hsforum.com/HeartSurgery/
LearningCtrHSF.html
```

Heart Disease and your health—what you should know. This page provides information and explanations of common cardiovascular diseases specifically for the non-medical audience.

Vegetarian Diets

```
http://www.fatfree.com/FAQ/ada-paper
```

This page contains a position paper by the American Dietetic Association. It states the Association's summary of the healthful nature of a vegetarian diet.

Injury Prevention

A Patient's Guide to Carpal Tunnel Syndrome

```
http://www.sechrest.com/mmg/cts/ctsintro.html
```

This page includes interesting information on the development and treatment of carpal tunnel syndrome.

Children's Safety Network

```
http://www.edc.org/HHD/csn/
```

This is a Web site for the National Injury and Violence Prevention Resource Center. Their goal is to provide resources and technical assistance to maternal and child health agencies and other organizations seeking to reduce unintentional injuries and violence to children and adolescents.

Emergency Medical Services

```
http://llama.thirdstreet.com/ems/
```

This page has fascinating facts and other helpful health information state-by-state, including suicide prevention.

First Aid On-Line

```
http://www.prairienet.org/~autumn/firstaid/
```

An excellent resource for what to do for common occurrences that need first aid.

GunInfo

```
http://www.guninfo.org/
```

Information to address the public's concern over gun-related injuries and deaths.

Head Injury Prevention and Rehabilitation

```
http://140.254.20.2/
```

part
2

Ohio Valley Center. This page is excellent!

Injury Control Resource Information Network

```
http://wwwdev.upmc.edu/icrin/
```

Excellent site for good information. It has about everything you could be looking for concerning injuries.

National Institute on Life Planning for People with Disabilities

```
http://www.sonic.net/nilp/
```

NILP is a national organization dedicated to promoting transition, life and person centered planning for all persons with disabilities and their families.

Trauma and Injury Prevention WWW Servers

```
http://rmstewart.uthscsa.edu/traumasites.html
```

More good injury prevention links!

Nutrition and Weight Control

The American Heart Association Diet

```
http://www.amhrt.org/pubs/ahadiet.html
```

This eating plan from the American Heart Association describes the latest advice of medical and nutritional experts. The best way to help lower your blood cholesterol is to eat less saturated fatty acids and cholesterol and control your weight. The AHA Diet gives you an easy-to-follow guide to eating with your heart in mind.

Arizona Health Sciences Library Nutrition Guide

```
http://www.medlib.arizona.edu/educ/nutrition.html
```

This is an extremely comprehensive page on most aspects of nutrition from the U. of Arizona.

Center for Science in the Public interest

```
http://www.cspinet.org/
```

A page designed to promote health by educating the public about nutrition and alcohol.

Electronic Gourmet Guide

```
http://www.foodwine.com/
```

This is a very tantalizing page with a lot of interesting information on food.

Fast Food Facts–Interactive Food Finder

```
http://www.olen.com/food/
```

This is a wonderful page designed to help anyone determine the ingredients of his or her favorite fast foods. Very interactive and useful.

Food and Nutrition: Selected Electronic Resources

```
http://www.nalusda.gov/fnic/
```

This is an excellent Web site that may be the first place to search for anything related to food and nutrition.

The Food Pyramid

```
http://www.ganesa.com/food/index.html
```

Up to date information on the latest information on what we used to know as the four food groups.

Health and Nutrition

```
http://dinnercoop.cs.cmu.edu/dinnercoop/special/
health.html
```

This is a page filled with nothing but more links to nutrition information around the world. It contains a very large number of links.

Human Health and Nutrition

`http://www.envirolink.org/arrs/health_wrap.html`

Animal Rights Resource Site. Contains information and links on nutrition and health that follows their philosophies.

Mother Nature's General Store

`http://www.mothernature.com/`

Forums, Libraries, Resources on nutrition and food. Page includes information on vitamins, herbs, recipes, and other interesting health information. I give this one a definite two thumbs up.

My Menus

`http://www.mymenus.com/`

The best recipe site on the Web! Thousands of nutritional recipes. Complete nutritional information. Instantly custom-build your own meal plans. Look up recipes by nutritional characteristic. YUMMY STUFF!

Nutribase On-Line

`http://www.nutribase.com`

This site features an interactive on-line database of over 19,000 food items and their associated nutrient information . . . food items that you can view, rank, query and search by food names. This database includes more than 3,000 menu items from over 70 restaurants. This site also features a weight-loss calculator, a calorie requirements calculator, "desirable" weight and body fat content charts, a directory of 1,400 food and supplement makers, a listing of healthy food substitutions, a glossary of foods and cooking terms, toll-free numbers for food makers, and 1,000 quotes and tips for dieters. It's all here!

Selected Fitness, Exercise, Nutrition, Food and Low Fat Recipe Sources

`http://www.idbsu.edu/carol/wellness.htm`

This is a page of useful links to many topics on wellness including a long list of excellent links to nutrition and weight control.

Veggies Unite!

`http://www.vegweb.com/`

This is a central site for all things vegetarian.

Public Health

The American Public Health Association

`http://www.apha.org/`

This is the homepage for the American Public Health Association which is one of the largest and most comprehensive public health organizations in the world.

NewsFile

`http://www.homepage.holowww.com/`

This site contains references and abstracts to journal articles that relate to public and community health. Excellent resource for research

The Virtual Public Health Center

`http://www-sci.lib.uci.edu/~martindale/PHealth.html`

Possibly the most comprehensive resource out there on public health.

Safety

Amazing Environmental Organization WebDirectory

`http://www.webdirectory.com/`

A huge directory of Web sites for all sorts of environmental subjects including those relating to safety.

Bicycle Helmet Safety Institute

`http://www.bhsi.org/index.htm`

This is a small, active, non-profit consumer-funded program acting as a clearinghouse and a technical resource for bicycle helmet information. Includes information on statistics, publications, laws, and advice on bicycle helmet safety as well as other helmet and bicycle type links.

Christie's Safety Related Internet Resources

```
http://www.mrg.ab.ca/christie/safelist.htm
```

Christie Communication services safety associations, large and small business, formal educational institutions, and government with educational information and training materials.

Consumer Product Safety Commission

```
gopher://cpsc.gov/
```

The U.S. Consumer Product Safety Commission (CPSC), is an independent federal regulatory agency that was created in 1972 by Congress in the Consumer Product Safety Act. This page is a Gopher server that contains lots of information and links regarding consumer product safety.

National Safety Council

```
http://206.55.43.11/
```

National Safety Council's mission is to educate and influence society to adopt safety, health and environmental policies, practices and procedures that prevent and mitigate human suffering and economic losses arising from preventable causes.

Product Safety Link Directory

```
http://www.safetylink.com/
```

This site has extensive information and links to many aspects of product safety.

Poisons Information Database

```
http://vhp.nus.sg/PID/
```

Information on natural toxins and poisons, and directories of antivenoms, toxicologists, and poison control centers around the world.

Safety Health Servers

```
http://www.midtown.net/~hcg/bookmrk.htm
```

This page contains links to a large list of safety and health resources.

U.S. Environmental Protection Agency

```
http://www.epa.gov/
```

This site contains a wealth of information about the agency and environmental issues as well as links to many other environmental and safety resources.

Self-Help and Self-Care

Cal Berkeley Wellness Letter

```
http://www.enews.com/magazines/ucbwl/
```

This Wellness Letter is edited by research scientists and written in lay English. Features the latest news from the world of preventive medicine and practical advice on all aspects of healthy living.

The Good Health Web

```
http://www.social.com/health/index.html
```

An excellent site with extensive links and information on health including, organizations, discussion groups, news, newsgroups, FAQ's, mailing lists, links to other sites and more.

Mental Health Net

```
http://www.cmhc.com/guide/substnce.htm
```

A comprehensive guide to mental health on-line featuring over 4,078 individual resources. This site has information on disorders such as depression, anxiety, panic attacks, chronic fatigue syndrome and substance abuse, in addition to professional resources in psychology, psychiatry and social work, journals and self-help magazines.

On-line Consumer Health Information

```
http://www.hirs.com/constemp.html
```

Contains extensive links and information sources for many topics related to consumer health.

The Other Revolution in Health Care

```
http://www.hotwired.com/wired/2.01/features/
healthcare.html
```

An interesting article on health care.

Patient/Consumer Health Information

```
http://www.kumc.edu/service/dykes/RRPAGES/patient/
phmpage.html
```

Lots of great information and sites for selected patient resources on many health-related topics that are available on the Internet.

Personal Development Sites

```
http://www.ns.net/~sjmoore/psites.html
```

Links to many journals, organizations, networks, businesses and other information sources dealing with personal development.

Psychology Self-Help Resources on the Internet

```
http://www.gasou.edu/psychweb/resource/selfhelp.htm
```

This site contains links to non-commercial sites providing information and help about specific disorders related to psychology. Excellent and extensive resources.

Self-Help

```
http://www.lib.ox.ac.uk/internet/news/faq/archive/
self-impr-faq.part1.html
```

Frequently asked questions on currently popular self-help resources such as NLP, speed reading, hypnosis amd many others. This is an excellent source of information on a huge list of topics.

Self-Help and Psychology Magazine

```
http://www.well.com/user/selfhelp/
```

A self-help resource that includes articles; self-help book reviews; movie reviews and software reviews for parents; questions and answers written by professionals; an interactive corner; cartoons; links, lists, and newsgroups spanning mental-health sites across the globe; a full-service bookstore; professional information and services, and much more.

Web Links for Medical and Mental Health Problems.

```
http://www.realtime.net/~mmjw/
```

An excellent source for many resources and links in many areas of medical and mental health. This site has been rated in the top 5% of all Web sites.

Stress Management

Create Your Own Hypnosis/Relaxation Tape

```
http://www.rahul.net/ndanger/hyptape.html
```

This is a page that teaches you all you need to know to create your own relaxation audio tape.

How to fight and conquer stress

```
http://www.coolware.com/health/joel/stress.html
```

This is an information page on stress as it affects us and some ideas on how to deal with it.

Introduction to Stress Management, NLP, and Hypnotherapy

```
http://www.bogo.co.uk/andys/index.html
```

This page includes a link to more good information on managing stress before it manages you.

StressFreeNET

`http://www.stressfree.com/`

StressFree Network is a system of Health Care professionals providing Solutions to Stress. They provide confidential assistance to individuals, business and occupational groups for whom stress is an important issue. They provide a continuum of wellness and stress related services; from diagnosis and assessment to implementation and solution. They provide solutions to stress.

The Web's Stress Management and Emotional Wellness Page

`http://imt.net/~randolfi/StressPage.html`

This is a great resource for stress management including some excellent links and ideas for managing stress.

part

2

Tobacco, Alcohol, and Drug Use

AIRSPACE Non-smokers' Rights Society

`http://www.seercom.com/airspace/`

AIRSPACE's goals are to require all indoor public places be smoke-free, to prohibit the sale of tobacco to minors, to prohibit all forms of tobacco promotion; and to hold the tobacco industry accountable for the disease and death caused by their product.

Al-Anon and Alateen

`http://www.Al-Anon-Alateen.org/`

AL-ANON (and ALATEEN for younger members) is a worldwide organization that offers a self-help recovery program for families and friends of alcoholics whether or not the alcoholic seeks help or even recognizes the existence of a drinking problem.

Alcohol Anonymous Resources.

`http://www.stattrax.com/cgi/reports.cgi/34:700:AAhome`

A collection of AA information. Information and links on many aspects of AA including, literature, history, intergroup phone numbers, meetings, conventions, computer programs, links to more AA related resources.

Center for Alcohol and Addiction Studies

```
http://center.butler.brown.edu/
```

Located at Brown University, the Center's mission is to promote the identification, prevention and effective treatment of alcohol and other drug use problems in our society through research, publications, education and training.

Drug-Related Network Resources

```
http://hyperreal.com/drugs/faqs/resources.html
```

This is a large list of links to many sites related to drugs of all types. Includes information on both sides of the controversies surrounding drugs.

National Clearinghouse for Alcohol and Drug Information

```
http://www.health.org/aboutn.htm
```

This is the information service of the Center for Substance Abuse Prevention of the U.S. Department of Health & Human Services. NCADI is the world's largest resource for current information and materials concerning substance abuse prevention.

National Institute on Drug Abuse

```
http://www.nida.nih.gov/
```

This Web site with information on the NIDA includes it's organizations, calendar of events, communications, grants and links to other related Web sites.

Smoking from All Sides

```
http://www.cs.brown.edu/people/lsh/smoking.html
```

Links to Web sites on many aspects of smoking including, health aspects, statistics, tobacco news, anti-smoking groups, smoking cessation, tobacco history, commentary, pro-smoking documents, smoking glamour, etc.

The Nicotine and Tobacco Network

```
http://ahsc.arizona.edu/nicnet
```

Great Resource from U. Of Arizona. Contains links and information on research, news, programs, resources and other items relating to nicotine and tobacco.

Violence Resources and Information

Assault Prevention Information Network

```
http://galaxy.tradewave.com/galaxy/Community/Safety/A
ssault-Prevention/apin/APINintro.html
```

This is an extensive Web site by Judith Weiss at "APIN" to begin a search for resources and sources related to the issue of violence. Web links and information for safety precautions, protecting children from violence, violence in the workplace, and stories, myths, and courses on self defense.

Domestic Violence in the Workplace

```
http://www.igc.apc.org/fund/workplace/
```

A Web site with articles, information and sites to many aspects of domestic violence.

National Crisis Prevention Institute's Violence Prevention Resource Center

```
http://www.execpc.com/~cpi/
```

CPI offers training in the safe management of disruptive and assaultive behavior, as well as other topics in areas such as business, mental health, corrections, security, police, youth and human services, and government.

National Institute for Occupational Safety and Health (NIOSH)

```
http://www.cdc.gov/niosh/homepage.html
```

NIOSH is a Federal agency established by the Occupational Safety and Health Act of 1970. NIOSH is part of the Centers for Disease Control and Prevention (CDC) and is responsible for conducting research and making recommendations for the prevention of work-related illness and injuries.

OSHA Guidelines for Workplace Violence Prevention Programs

http://www.osha.gov/oshpubs/

This site contains several articles relating to worksite violence.

Satore Township

http://www.crl.com/~mikekell/index.html

This page has been rated in the top 5% of all Web pages. It is an information page dealing with violence and homicide in the workplace. It has excellent references to workplace violence information, resources and publications.

The Rockem-Sockem Workplace

http://venable.com/wlu/rockem.htm

This is an informative article on violence in the workplace.

Violence at Work and School

http://galaxy.tradewave.com/editors/weiss/WorkSD.html

A large collection of sites regarding violence prevention from the Assault Prevention Information Network.

Wellness and Optimum Health

Articles on Wellness and Financial Well-being

http://www.ns.net/cash/c_art.html

This page includes information on the links between money, health, productivity, stress, self-esteem, and overall well-being.

part
2

The Cyberspace Wellness Center

```
http://www.telemedical.com/~drcarr/Telemedical/
cws.html
```

This center is a place to receive wellness information and services. It is an excellent resource.

The Mind/Body Medical Institute at Harvard Medical School

```
http://www.med.harvard.edu/programs/mindbody/
```

Resource page to the Mind/Body Clinic. Extensive information.

National Wellness Institute

```
http://wellness.uwsp.edu/scripts/Health_Service/
WebImage/WebImage.exe
```

This is the homepage for the National Wellness Institute including the many departments and conferences associated with it.

Women's Health

Altanta Reproductive Health Centre

```
http://www.ivf.com/
```

Excellent resources for topics of interest to women. One of the best out there.

Breastfeeding Articles and Resources

```
http://www.parentsplace.com/readroom/bf.html
```

This page includes articles and information on nearly every question anyone could ever ask regarding breastfeeding.

MedWeb Gynecology and women's health

```
http://www.gen.emory.edu/medweb/medweb.gynecology.
html
```

Excellent resource with extensive links to a great number of women's medical and health issues.

Natural Progesterone and Women's Health

```
http://www.health-science.com/health.htm
```

This is a page with information on PMS, fertility, menopause, osteoporosis, and other women's health topics.

Planned Parenthood

```
http://www.ppfa.org/ppfa/index.html
```

Resources on sexual and reproductive health.

Sexual Assault Information

```
http://www.cs.utk.edu/~bartley/saInfoPage.html
```

This page includes a nice search for many subtopics falling under the main topic of sexual assault. This is an excellent reference.

Women's' Health America Group

```
http://www1.fourlakes.net/~wha/
```

Dynamic national organization whose mission is to encourage and enable women to make informed decisions about their healthcare by providing access to current and accurate information and quality health products.

Web Activities

In this section you will find some activities that will help you use the health-related Internet Web sites in interesting and creative ways. Each of the activities will help you become more familiar with the Internet. They will also help you learn interesting and unique ways to find excellent health information. These activities correspond with the health topic areas in the Address Book section of this text. You may find it helpful to refer back to these sections while doing the activities.

Activity One–Health News

Something wonderful about the Internet is the speed that information travels to and from all parts of the world. What formerly took weeks and months to learn about the newest research and developments in health are now available almost immediately. This activity will help you understand how this works.

Using the Health News pages, try to see how many news articles or news clips you can find that have come out in the past week or two on the topic of heart disease. Try to see how many of those news stories discuss modes of treatment, how many describe ways to prevent heart disease, and how many discuss risk factors for heart disease.

Do the same exercise for the following topics:

Cancer

HIV/AIDS

Diabetes

Health-Related Searches

This exercise will help you to become more proficient at using the search engines to your advantage. Using at least four of the health directed search engines work on the following exercises. Sexually transmitted diseases are a major health concern. Using the search engines below find pages that give up-to-date information on the various types of sexually transmitted diseases that are common today. Look for current information on the following for each of the STDs:

Signs and symptoms

Incubation periods of each

Prevalence

Treatment—which are curable, which aren't and how the curable are cured

Prevention

For extra points, find pages with pictures of the various STDs, download them and include them in your graphics folder on your computer to be used in your next report on sexually transmitted diseases.

Health-Related Journals, Magazines and Periodicals

The next time one of your teachers gives you an assignment to do a health report, try to draw primarily from these on-line periodicals listed in the section of Journals, Magazines, and Periodicals. Do not use them exclusively but try to gather your information predominantly from these. See if the quality of the content of your paper is as good as the quality of those who use regular magazines, journals, and books to do theirs.

Alternative Medicine and Holistic Health

This exercise will help you gain a greater understanding of non-traditional or alternative forms of health and healing. In western medicine, we commonly treat headaches by taking an aspirin or some other type of pain reliever. However, there are other ways of treating the same problem without the use of drugs such as biofeedback, massage, acupressure or herbs. Using the Web sites listed below, find several alternative forms of therapy other than the traditional western medicine mode of treatment for the following ailments:

Muscle pain

Arthritis

Constipation

Stress

Cancer

Heart Disease

Others _____________________

Cancer

This exercise will help you become more acquainted with cancer information.

Try to find answers to the following questions using the Web sites in the Cancer section:

Which type of cancer is the most prevalent in our society?

Which cancer has the greatest recovery rate?

Which type of cancer is usually the most painful?

Why is lung cancer such a dangerous form of cancer?

What are the best ways for women to decrease their risk of breast cancer?

What are the best ways for men to decrease their risk of prostate cancer?

What are the conventional and unconventional methods of cancer treatment?

Are there behavioral activities that can reduce one's risk of certain cancers?

Community Health

This exercise will help you gather current information on community health issues that face our society. Use the Web sites in the Community Health Section of addresses to find the following information:

Which states in the country have the highest rates for the following:
- percentage of the population who exercise
- percentage who smoke
- percentage who are either overweight or obese
- number of AIDS cases by state

Comparing men and women, describe the cancer incidence and cancer deaths by sites in the body (e.g. breast, colon, lung).

How healthy is the water we drink and air we breathe in different parts of the country?

What are the leading causes of death in the U.S. for the following age groups:
- infants
- children
- adolescents
- young adults
- adults
- elderly

Diseases: Chronic and Acute

These exercises will help you learn more about other diseases that are common in our society. Use the disease related Web sites to find the answers to the following questions:

What are the common respiratory diseases in our society?

What are the common signs and symptoms of respiratory diseases?

What are the main causes for these types of diseases?

What treatments are available for respiratory diseases?

What are some common congenital diseases in our society?

What are causes and treatments for these?

How does the immune system work?

Using a metaphor, such as the sport of football, describe the immune system. Give the different parts of the immune system names that would apply in the sport of football. For example, the defensive line might be the T or B lymphocytes. What part of the immune system would be the linebackers? What about the tight end, the defensive backs and the cornerbacks? Would the coaches play a role? How would the offensive positions on a football team represent other parts of the immune system? Be creative.

part

2

Environmental Health

Using the environmental health Web sites try to find answers to the following questions:

What is the ozone layer?
What is the current state of the ozone?

What are some common ways that we contaminate our water supply?
What does the Safe Drinking Water Act of 1974 say?

What are the most common sources of smog or air pollution
   in most cities?
What are some common health effects of smog or air pollution?

Exercise and Fitness

Using information available from the following exercise and fitness Web sites, find out the following information about your own fitness levels:

Determine your aerobic exercise training zone based on your heart rate.

What are the recommended guidelines for aerobic activity for you?

Using the Internet, develop a complete conditioning program that includes stretching and flexibility, weight training, aerobic activities, and high intensity workouts for the following people:

- A track person who runs the 100 or 220 meters
- A basketball player
- A marathon runner
- A non-athlete who wants to lose 10 pounds and become more fit

Find out what are the major differences and similarities between each of these conditioning regimens?

General Health

Using the Web sites in the General Health section, find an on-line **personal health risk appraisal.** Find out your general levels of health including risk factors for diseases, problem areas, and areas where you are particularly strong. Record this information and compare it to health risk appraisals you have completed in the past. How do you compare?

Government and Non-Government Health Resources and Databases

Here is an activity designed to help you find information on virtually any health-related *organization* in this country and many others around the world. If you are unaware of where to begin your search, there are several Web sites that have started the process for you. The first one is: **http://nhic-nt.health.org/**

Once there, click on the words "Toll free numbers for health information." Immediately you will see an enormous list of health-related organizations. Clicking on any of these will bring up an information page on that specific organization including how to contact them toll free.

Another page that has health organizations categorized by state is at this address: **http://www.social.com/health/nhic/data/index.html**

You will probably find what you are looking for by choosing the yahoo search for health associations. The address for this is: **http://www.yahoo.com/Health/Organizations**

With these three sites and a small investment of time, you can easily find information on just about any common, and some uncommon, health organizations that exist. You may also simply type in the words "health" and "organization" in the text box of any of your favorite search engines.

Health and Disease Care

In the Web pages in the Health and Disease Care section, and using the Health-Related Search Engines, find the main similarities and differences between the following basic types of health insurance plans:

- private insurance
- health maintenance organizations
- preferred provider organizations

Which of these health insurance plans seems to make the most sense for the majority of Americans today?

Which makes most sense for you in your current situation?

Health Education

As you look through the Health Education Web sites, try to find some answers to the following questions:

Why is prevention the best approach to impacting the quality of health in the United States?

In what ways can a health educator play a key role in the prevention approach to health care?

Health Promotion

There is currently some question regarding the term "Health Promotion." It is a popular term but not everyone agrees on its scope. Based on these health promotion Web sites and the links that come from these sites to other health promotion Web sites, answer the following questions:

How would you define health promotion?

What are some major hurdles that must be overcome in health promotion?

What types of activities are recommended to encorporate health promotion in the worksites?

What are some benefits in terms of economics and personal health of worksite health promotion?

Health Psychology

What is your greatest fear? Search through the health psychology pages to see if the fear has a name. (Example: fear of open spaces—agoraphobia)

A basic principle in health psychology, and for that matter, individual self development is that of modeling. Modeling means if we want to become very good at something, one of the quickest ways of getting there is to find someone else who has succeeded in doing that thing and do the same things he or she did. This can be especially useful for the beginning or intermediate health educator or other health profession students. A nice activity designed to help you clarify where you want to go professionally follows a format something like this: (For this activity you will need a pen and a paper at first.)

1. Think of an area in health that interests you and write it down. (This may be quite broad such as fitness, or it may be more detailed such as a weight control specialist.)

2. Think of a setting that you would like to be working in once you are finished with your degree and write it down. (The majority of the health settings where health professionals work include the following: the worksite, the medical setting, the community, the school, or the university. There are many variations among these main settings.)

3. Think of how you might be working in that setting. What would you like your major roles to be? Write these down. (This might include something like managing a staff of aerobic instructors as part of a worksite health promotion program.)

4. Think of some ways you may be involved in assessing the needs of the setting. (How might you determine the types of health-related activities and programs that will be appropriate for this particular setting?)

5. Think of some ways you may evaluate the effectiveness of your program. (For example, if it is a weight loss program, what amount of weight will the people need to lose and over how much time will they have to keep the pounds off in order for you to feel like your program is successful?)

Now, having generated these thoughts in your mind, your next step is to find the people who are doing the same things and learn what they did to get there and why they are successful at doing what they do. This is where the Internet can be a very valuable tool. Some starting places in this search might include the following: **http://userwww.service.emory. edu/~cescoff/cam.html**

This page contains excellent information regarding the profession of health education. This includes professional certification, Health Education and Promotion Listservs or discussion groups, and State Health Addresses on the Internet. By subscribing to one of the listservs or accessing one of the professional organizations, you can quickly bring yourself into contact with many health professionals. You may also use any of your favorite search engines and type in the words "health" and "professional preparation." See what results come up and scroll through them. Once you find the person, there is usually a place where you can contact them using either E-mail, snail mail or even a phone call. Finding the experts and the successful people in your field is that easy.

Heart Health

This exercise will help you become more acquainted with the number one killer in our society—heart disease. Answer the following questions using the heart health Web sites:

What are the various types of heart disease?

Can you find the average dollar costs of the various types of treatment currently available for heart disease?

What is angina pectoris?

In what ways does stress relate to heart disease?

How does a stroke differ from a heart attack?

Are there behavioral activities that can reduce one's risk of heart disease?

Injury Prevention

Do you know what to do if someone begins bleeding? What if someone begins to have a pain in their chest and down their left side? How do you respond to someone who has a tick stuck in their leg or has swallowed some poison? Look through the Injury Prevention pages to find the answers to these and many other questions relating to first aid and injury prevention.

Nutrition and Weight Control

For this exercise, first think of your favorite dinner at your favorite fast food restaurant. Write down each item on a piece of paper (For example: a Wendy's Double with cheese, biggie fries, large frostie, and a cookie). Using the Nutrition and Weight Control Web pages find the following information:

What is the total number of calories for the meal?

What is the total number of fat calories for the meal?

What is the total number of saturated fat calories?

What is the percentage of fat calories for the meal?

What is the percentage of saturated fat calories?

What is the total number of simple sugar (simple carbohydrate) calories?

Next, find out what the recommendations are for healthy nutrition considering both fat intake and simple sugar intake.

How does your meal stack up with the recommendations?

Public Health

Here is a little activity that will thoroughly amaze you. I promise. First type in the following Web site in your browser's URL window: http://www-sci.lib.uci.edu/~martindale/PHealth.html This Web site is called *The Virtual Public Health Center.*

You will find that you can easily spend a few minutes or a few hours at this one location. Just look through all the variety of activities and information relating not only to public health, but to a host of other subjects that are health-related. This is one of the finest Web sites out there. Stop in for a visit. You will not be disappointed!

Safety

Try to find information that will help you determine if you have anything in your home that puts someone's safety at risk based on the information from the Safety Web sites. What recommendations can you find for making sure the products you buy are safe? What about your school or work? Are there ways to increase the safety of these places suggested by these safety Web sites?

Self-Help and Self-Care

Going through the Web pages in the Self-Help & Self-Care section, list the 20 best things you can do for yourself on an ongoing basis to maintain and enhance your personal sense of health and well-being. These self-help Web sites will give you some ideas that perhaps you had not considered.

Prioritize them in order of importance to you.

Keeping a notebook handy, write down everything you do (every single activity) at the end of each day for two weeks.

At the end of those two weeks compare your daily activities with the items on the list. See if you are spending very much time involved in those things that you consider the most important. (Some people say that the difference between the two lists is proportional to the amount of stress we feel.) Make changes in your activities so you are spending more time doing the things that are most important to you and say "no" more often to those things that you do quite frequently but are not on your list.

Stress Management

Follow the instructions on the first Web site in the Stress Management section and create your own personal relaxation tape. The URL is: **http://www.rahul.net/ndanger/hyptape.html**

Spend 15 minutes each day practicing relaxation using your tape. Write down your experiences of how your days go while you spend time each day to really relax. Compare these days with days that you don't spend a few minutes relaxing. Notice the differences.

Tobacco, Alcohol, and Drug Use

Use the sites in the Tobacco, Alcohol, and Drug Use section to determine the differences between a chemical dependencey, an addiction, a habit, and a preference in relation to tobacco, alcohol, and drugs.

Based on your body weight, find a Web site that will give you information on how many drinks it takes for you to reach certain blood alcohol levels. What are the effects on your driving ability of drinking that many drinks.

Find out the most effective ways to quit smoking according to Web sites on the Internet. (You may find this information in the Tobacco, Alcohol, and Drug Use Web sites or by using the search engines that were presented earlier.) How many different ways are there? If you or someone you know smokes, how many ways of quitting have you or they tried? How effective were those methods for quitting?

Violence Resources and Information

Using the Web sites in this section, describe some recommendations for reducing violence in the workplace. Think about your own environment including your neighborhood, family, school, or workplace.

What amount of violence exists in these places?

According to these Web pages, what can you do to reduce your risks of being a victim of violence?

What do they suggest that you can do to help decrease the amount of violence in your environments?

Wellness and Optimum Health

You have just been asked to write an article on high-level wellness for a major newspaper. Based on the information in the Wellness and Optimum Health Web pages (you may also use the health-related search engines for additional assistance) what characteristics or qualities would you say are important for the person striving for high level-wellness? Who are some models that you would include in your article to use as examples of people who demonstrate high-level wellness? Write your article and submit it to your local or school paper.

Women's Health

Using the Women's Health Web sites, find five health concerns that are specific to women? How do these Web sites address those health concerns?

Do you know of someone who has been sexually assaulted? What advice or suggestions do the Web sites in this section give to those who have been assaulted? Can this information be useful at the present time for this person? If so, in what ways?

part

2

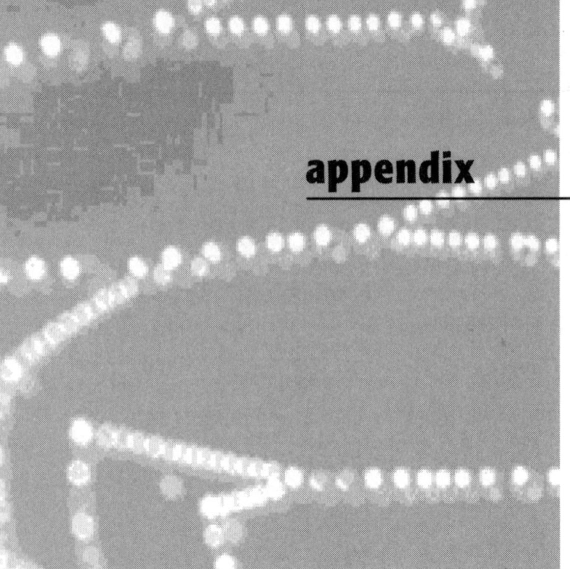

List of URLs (Web Addresses)

Health News

http://www.achoo.com/newspage/index.htm
http://www.eatright.org/pressindex.html
http://www.chronicillnet.org/online/
http://www.cnn.com/HEALTH/index.html
    http://www.com/healthnews/
http://healthnet.ivi.com/ivi/mayo/common/htm/newsstnd.htm
http://www.newspage.com/NEWSPAGE/cgi-
    bin/walk.cgi/NEWSPAGE/info/d15/
http://www.reutershealth.com/
http://www.newstimes.com/news/today/health.htm
http://167.8.29.13/life/health/lhd1.htm
http://www.wellmedia.com/news.html
http://www.yahoo.com/headlines/health/
http://nytsyn.com/med/

Health-Related Searches

http://www.altavista.digital.com/
http://www.webdirectory.com/Health/
http://www.excite.com/Subject/Health_and_Medicine/s-index.h.html
http://www.einet.net/galaxy/Community/Health.html
http://www.HealthAtoZ.com/
http://guide-p.infoseek.com//DB?tid=1207&db=0&sv=IS&lk=noframes
http://www.linkmonster.com/health.html
http://a2z.lycos.com/Health_and_Medicine/

http://www.mckinley.com/browse_bd.cgi?Health
http://www.medexplorer.com/
http://www.kumc.edu:80/mmatrix/
http://www.pointcom.com/categories/health/
http://www.stpt.com/
http://vh.radiology.uiowa.edu/Misc/Search.html
http://www.webcrawler.com/select/med.new.html
http://www.yahoo.com/Health/

Health-Related journals, magazines and periodicals

http://www.allabouthealth.com/
http://www.forthrt.com/~chronicl/homepage.html
http://carlisle-www.army.mil/apfri/alive.htm
http://ww2.hyperlink.com/balance/
http://www.hinman.oro.net/~bmsweb/bmsmag.htm
http://www.cdc.net/~primus/fpc/fpcjs70.htm#10
http://www.lifelines.com/lifenews.html
http://healthnet.ivi.com/ivi/mayo/common/htm/library.htm
http://www.dash.com/netro/nwx/tmr/tmr.html
http://www.medscape.com/
http://mensfitness.com/
http://www.newfrontier.com/
http://www.newage.com/
http://www.nejm.org/ http://www.cspinet.org/nah/
http://pie.org/E21221T3783
http://www.shareguide.com/mag/
http://www.thorne.com/townsend.html
http://nansen.jhuapl.edu/wej/
http://www.yogajournal.com

Alternative Medicine and Holistic Health

http://sunsite.sut.ac.jp/arch/academic/medicine/alternative-healthcare/
http://www.Acupuncture.com/ http://www.pitt.edu/~cbw/altm.html
http://www.quake.net/~xdcrlab/hp.html http://sunsite.unc.edu/herbs/
http://www.tiac.net/users/mgold/health.html
http://www.nursery.com/~interlud/links.htm
http://www.gen.emory.edu/MEDWEB/keyword/alternative_medicine.
    html
http://www.spiritweb.org/
http://www.teleport.com/~amrta/
http://www.oxytherapy.com/

http://zeta.cs.adfa.oz.au/Spirituality.html
http://ezinfo.ucs.indiana.edu/~aeulenbe/i_see
http://wellmedia.com/links.html

Cancer

http://www.cancer.org/
http://nysernet.org/bcic/
http://www.cancernews.com/
http://www.access.digex.net/~mkragen/cansearch.html
http://africa.com/~martin/jomol/ http://www.nci.nih.gov/
http://www.cancer.med.umich.edu/NCCN/NCCN.html
http://www.maui.net/~southsky/introto.html http://cancerguide.org/
http://www.oncolink.upenn.edu/

Community Health

http://www.amhrt.org/
http://www.cdc.gov/cdc.html
http://web.indstate.edu/hlthsfty/hlth221/chhome.htm
http://userwww.service.emory.edu/~cescoff/cam.html
http://www.health.org/
http://www.homepage.holowww.com/
http://www.paho.org/
http://www.who.ch/

Diseases: Chronic and Acute

http://a2z.lycos.com/Health_and_Medicine/Illnesses_and_Disorders/
http://www.diabetes.org/
http://www.lungusa.org/noframes/
http://www.cdc.gov/diseases/diseases.html
http://www.chronicillnet.org/
http://www.mic.ki.se/Diseases/index.html
http://www.kumc.edu/service/dykes/RRPAGES/patient/pchronic.html
http://medhlp.netusa.net/
http://ftp.cdc.gov/nccdphp/nccdhome.htm
http://www.sig.net/~allergy/welcome.html
http://point.lycos.com/reviews/database/hmil_e.html
http://www.bocklabs.wisc.edu/Welcome.html

Environmental Health

http://atsdr1.atsdr.cdc.gov:8080/cx.html
http://clas.www.pdx.edu/~willert/EnvHealth.html

http://www.cdc.gov/nceh/0ncehhom.htm
http://www.niehs.nih.gov/
http://www.pacificrim.net/~nature/

Exercise and Fitness

http://www.aahperd.org/
http://www.a1.com/sportsmed/
http://www.etc.bc.ca/~dsamulak/
ftp://ftp.cray.com/pub/misc.fitness/misc.fitness.faq.html
http://hyrax.med.uth.tmc.edu/ptnt/00000384.htm
http://www.sportlink.com/fitness/
http://www.fitnessworld.com/
http://www.welltech.com/net_connect/fit.html
http://www.noah.cuny.edu/pregnancy/march_of_dimes/pre_preg.plan/
    fit42is.html
http://www.comlab.ox.ac.uk/oucl/users/sharon.curtis/BigFolks/fitres_
    FAQ.html
http://www.cdc.net/~primus/fpc/fpchome.html
http://www.kin.ucalgary.ca/isb/index.html
http://www.umich.edu/~divkines/kinesworld/
http://www.ncppa.org/
http://sunsite.unc.edu/drears/running/running.html
http://www.cs.huji.ac.il/papers/rma/stretching_toc.html
http://www.cs.unc.edu/~kyle/weights.html
http://fiat.gslis.utexas.edu/~lewisa/womsprt.html
http://www.worldguide.com/Fitness/hf.html

General Health

http://h-devil-www.mc.duke.edu/h-devil
http://www.localweb.com/gateway/
http://galaxy.einet.net/galaxy/Community/Health.html
http://www.cc.columbia.edu:80/cu/healthwise/
http://www.arcade.uiowa.edu/hardin-www/md.html
http://www.healthtouch.com/
http://www.northwesternmutual.com/longevit/longevit.htm
http://www.vix.com/men/health/health.html
http://www.ncahf.org/
http://www.nih.gov http://nhic-nt.health.org/
http://www.ihr.com/topics.html
http://www.stayhealthy.com/
http://www.yahoo.com/Health

Governmental Health Resources and Databases

http://www.ncsl.org/ihpp/
http://atl1.mercer.edu/www/health/health.html
http://www.ljextra.com/practice/health/hegov.html
http://wwwonder.cdc.gov/
http://www.cdc.gov/epo/mmwr/mmwr.html
http://www.cdc.gov/nchswww/nchshome.htm

Health and Disease Care

http://www.AmHPI.com/
http://www.amso.com/
http://www.convergentmedical.com/
http://www.globalmedic.com/
http://www.wp.com/HCLA/
http://www.microserve.net/~csi/HealthLinks.HTML
http://www.life-line.org/site1.cgi
http://www5.medscape.com/Home/About.mhtml#Mission
http://www.opuscomm.com/
http://www.ihr.com/natlorg.html

Health Education

http://www.cancer.org/cshe.html
http://www.ericsp.org/hprdtoc.html
http://www.ex.ac.uk/~dregis/healthy.html
http://www.nyu.edu/education/health/healthed/taub/hepr/frames/
    index.html

Health Promotion

http://www.awhp.com/
http://www.monash.edu.au/health/
http://www.siu.edu/~crhssd/rhres.htm
http://www.welltech.com/

Health Psychology

http://www.apa.org
http://www.athealth.com/
http://www.shef.ac.uk/~psysc/psychotherapy/index.html
http://www.uwsp.edu/acad/psych/dk/danielpg.htm
http://www.coil.com/~grohol/
http://fly.hiwaay.net/~garson/

http://www.gen.emory.edu/MEDWEB/keyword/mental_health~
    psychiatry~psychology.h
tml http://www.cmhc.com/
http://pie.org/E18634T3783
http://www.psyunix.iupui.edu/psych_dir.html
http://www.cloud9.net/~thorpy/

Heart Health

http://www.cardio.com/articles/preventn.htm
http://www.cardio.com/
http://sln.fi.edu/biosci/healthy/healthy.html
http://www.iea.com/~tcantre/education.html
http://www.hsforum.com/heartsurgery/home.hsf
http://www.mindspring.com/~mtm/news.html
http://www.internetwks.com/pauling/
http://www.hsforum.com/HeartSurgery/LearningCtrHSF.html
http://www.fatfree.com/FAQ/ada-paper

Injury Prevention

http://www.sechrest.com/mmg/cts/ctsintro.html
http://www.edc.org/HHD/csn/
http://llama.thirdstreet.com/ems/
http://www.prairienet.org/~autumn/firstaid/ http://www.guninfo.org/
http://140.254.20.2/
http://wwwdev.upmc.edu/icrin/
http://www.sonic.net/nilp/
http://rmstewart.uthscsa.edu/traumasites.html

Nutrition and Weight Control

http://www.amhrt.org/pubs/ahadiet.html
http://www.medlib.arizona.edu/educ/nutrition.html
http://www.cspinet.org/
http://www.foodwine.com/
http://www.olen.com/food/
http://www.nalusda.gov/fnic/
http://www.ganesa.com/food/index.html
http://dinnercoop.cs.cmu.edu/dinnercoop/special/health.html
http://www.envirolink.org/arrs/health_wrap.html
http://www.mothernature.com/
http://www.mymenus.com/
http://www.nutribase.com

http://www.idbsu.edu/carol/wellness.htm
http://www.vegweb.com/

Public Health

http://www-sci.lib.uci.edu/~martindale/PHealth.html
http://www.homepage.holowww.com/

Safety

http://www.webdirectory.com/
http://www.bhsi.org/index.htm
http://www.mrg.ab.ca/christie/safelist.htm
gopher://cpsc.gov/
http://206.55.43.11 http://www.safetylink.com/
http://vhp.nus.sg/PID/
http://www.midtown.net/~hcg/bookmrk.htm
http://www.epa.gov/

Self-Help & Self-Care

http://www.enews.com/magazines/ucbwl/
http://www.social.com/health/index.html
http://www.cmhc.com/guide/substnce.htm
http://www.hirs.com/constemp.html
http://www.hotwired.com/wired/2.01/features/healthcare.html
http://www.kumc.edu/service/dykes/RRPAGES/patient/phmpage.html
http://www.ns.net/~sjmoore/psites.html
http://www.gasou.edu/psychweb/resource/selfhelp.htm
http://www.lib.ox.ac.uk/internet/news/faq/archive/
     self-impr-faq.part1.html
http://www.well.com/user/selfhelp/
http://www.realtime.net/~mmjw/

Stress Management

http://www.rahul.net/ndanger/hyptape.html
http://www.coolware.com/health/joel/stress.html
http://www.bogo.co.uk/andys/index.html
http://www.stressfree.com/
http://imt.net/~randolfi/StressPage.html

Tobacco, Alcohol and Drug use

http://www.seercom.com/airspace/
http://www.Al-Anon-Alateen.org/

http://www.stattrax.com/cgi/reports.cgi/34:700:AAhome
http://center.butler.brown.edu/
http://hyperreal.com/drugs/faqs/resources.html
http://www.health.org/aboutn.htm
http://www.nida.nih.gov/
http://www.cs.brown.edu/people/lsh/smoking.html
http://ahsc.arizona.edu/nicnet

Violence Resources and Information

http://galaxy.tradewave.com/galaxy/Community/Safety/
  Assault-Prevention/apin/APINintro.html
http://www.igc.apc.org/fund/workplace/
http://www.execpc.com/~cpi/
http://www.cdc.gov/niosh/homepage.html
http://www.osha.gov/oshpubs/
http://www.crl.com/~mikekell/index.html
http://venable.com/wlu/rockem.htm
http://galaxy.tradewave.com/editors/weiss/WorkSD.html

Wellness and Optimum Health

http://www.ns.net/cash/c_art.html
http://www.telemedical.com/~drcarr/Telemedical/cws.html
http://www.med.harvard.edu/programs/mindbody/
http://wellness.uwsp.edu/scripts/Health_Service/WebImage/
  WebImage.exe

Women's Health

http://www.ivf.com/
http://www.parentsplace.com/readroom/bf.html
http://www.gen.emory.edu/medweb/medweb.gynecology.html
http://www.health-science.com/health.htm
http://www.ppfa.org/ppfa/index.html
http://www.cs.utk.edu/~bartley/saInfoPage.html
http://www1.fourlakes.net/~wha/

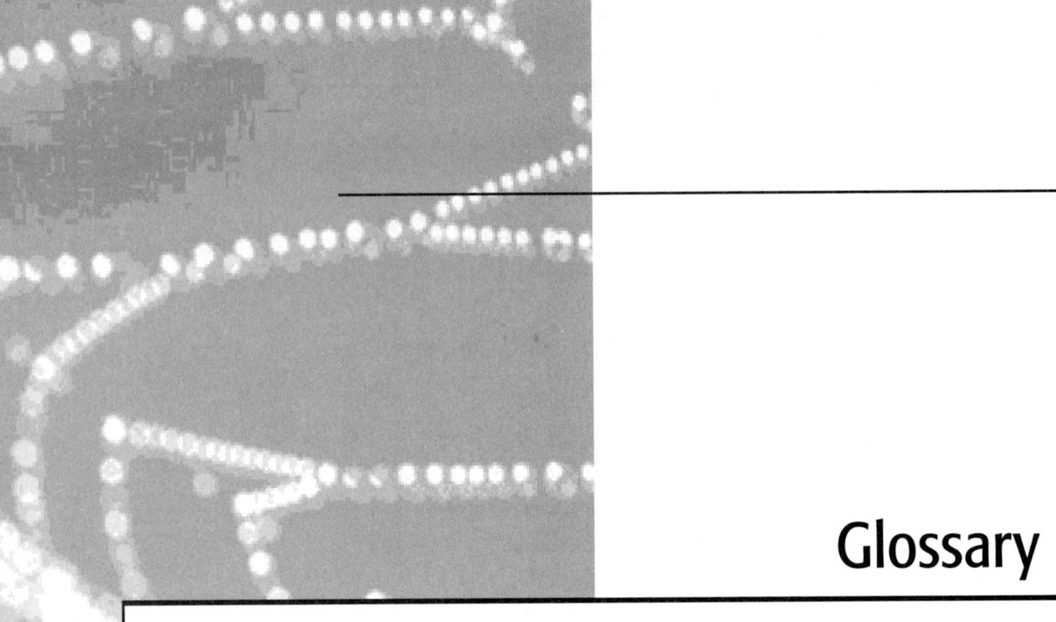

Glossary

browser
The computer program that lets you view the contents of Web sites.

cross post
Simultaneously send a message to more than one *newsgroup*.

digest
A compilation of several messages posted to an Internet *newsgroup*, sent to subscribers as a single message.

download
Copying a file from another computer to your computer over the Internet.

emoticon
A number of characters (usually punctuation) typed together to make a picture. For example, a smiley face is written as the emoticon shown below.

:-)

E-mail
Electronic mail.

FAQ
Frequently Asked Questions.

flame

A rude or derogatory message directed as a personal attack against an individual or group.

flame war

An exchange of flames (see above).

home page

A page on the World Wide Web that acts as a starting point for information about a person or organization.

hypertext

Text that contains embedded *links* to other pages of text. Hypertext enables the reader to navigate between pages of related information by following links in the text.

link

A reference to a location on the Web that is embedded in the text of Web page. Links are usually highlighted with a different color or underline to make them easily visible.

list

A mechanism for automatically sending *E-mail* messages to a group of subscribers.

listserver

A computer program that manages a *list*.

lurker

A passive reader of an Internet *newsgroup*. A lurker reads messages, but does not participate in the discussion by posting or responding to messages.

newbie

A new user of the Internet.

newsgroup

A discussion forum in which all participants can read all messages and public replies between the participants.

post
When used as a verb, "post" means to send a message. When used as a noun, "post" is a synonym for "message."

search engine
A computer program that will locate Web sites or files based on specified criterion.

spam
Spam is to the Internet as unsolicited junk mail is to the postal system.

thread
A series of messages in which a discussion is carried out.

URL
Uniform Resource Locator: The notation for specifying Web page addresses (e.g., http://www.aba con.com).

Usenet
The section of the Internet that is devoted to *newsgroups*.